I NEVER SAW MY FATHER AGAIN

THE DIVORCE COURT EFFECT

BY JORYN JENKINS

CHANGING THE WAY THE WORLD GETS DIVORCED?

OPEN PALM PRESS

This work is based on actual clients and their dissolutions of marriage. I've tried to recreate events and conversations from memory. Names and identifying details have been changed to protect the privacy of the individuals. Because of the dynamic nature of the Internet, any Web addresses or links referenced in this book may have changed since publication and may no longer be valid.

Although the author and publisher have made every effort to ensure that the information in this book was correct at press time, the author and publisher do not assume and hereby disclaim any liability to any party for any loss, damage, or disruption caused by errors or omissions, whether such errors or omissions result from negligence, accident, or any other cause.

I Never Saw My Father Again

First Printing: July 2015
Printed in the United States of America

First Edition: July 2015

Dedication

I dedicate this book to the people who find themselves at the end of certain relationships, whether they be marital, corporate, partnership, employment, or yet some other form of marriage. May you find peace during this transition, restructure that relationship with success, and discover joy in the next chapter of your life.

Acknowledgments

Self-help books like this one are never written alone. Like my first book, *War or Peace*, this manuscript was a long time in gestation and required a multitude of midwives to deliver it . . . three and a half decades and countless clients.

During those years, my clients lived through the wars and the negotiations presented here as though they were simple stories. It's easy to imagine they are fictional, but they are not; the events depicted happened to real people who grieved, stressed, suffered, agonized, and wept.

These events also happened to their children, some of whom are grown now and have children of their own. And some of whom have come to me for advice about *their* divorces.

It is to these parents and their children that I owe a huge debt. They inspire me to continue the quest every day to change the way the world gets divorced.

Advance Praise for I Never Saw My Father Again

Joryn Jenkins' *I Never Saw My Father Again* makes clear that individuals destined for dissolution can be masters of their own destiny by using modern resolution tools to stay out of the courtroom. Family Law practitioners and parents alike have a responsibility to children to settle issues and avoid the emotional and financial devastation of litigation. There is a new way of getting through this process. Jenkins' book helps explain why and how the evolution is necessary for our generation.

– Laura A. Wasser, divorce attorney to the stars, author of *It Doesn't Have to Be That Way: How to Divorce Without Destroying Your Family or Bankrupting Yourself*

In her book, *I Never Saw My Father Again*, Joryn Jenkins tells the personal toll divorce took in her life that set her on the path to becoming a divorce attorney. She shares her professional legal wisdom and experience for pursuing the collaborative divorce, or what I, as a marriage therapist, call "the good divorce." Make it your survival guide for navigating the process with respect and integrity so you can avoid the high cost, both financial and emotional, that those going through divorce often pay, especially the children.

– Dr. Jane Greer, psychotherapist and relationship expert, and author of *What About Me? Stop Selfishness From Ruining Your Relationship* marriage and family therapist, sex expert, author, radio host, and creator of the popular celebrity sex & relationship commentary, *Shrink Wrap with Dr. Jane Greer*

Joryn Jenkins' *I Never Saw My Father Again* is a perfect follow-up to *War or Peace*, her unflinching portrayal of the unpredictable, and often arbitrary, results when parents turn decisions involving their children over to the court system. If contested divorces and custody lawsuits are a betrayal of our children, the collaborative process is a gift to them. Jenkins makes the case for parents and children. She outlines the collaborative process in great detail, and explains how it works for both lay people and attorneys. This is a must-read for parents who are deciding how they want to restructure their relationships and their children's lives upon divorce. For attorneys, the collaborative way should be the very first choice for our clients, and Jenkins' makes the winning argument for why we need to re-direct our practices to the collaborative way.

> **– Mary Ann Young, former litigator, current mediator and collaborative lawyer, in practice since 1979, AV rated by Martindale Hubbell in 1996**

Joryn once again delivers an important resource for families facing divorce. She begins by discussing an important truth: families don't belong in the courtroom. She then not only describes the skeletal structure of the collaborative divorce process in a logical, well thought out manner, but adds living flesh to those bones by telling the stories of real people. She also draws upon her own life experiences to further enrich her narrative. If you are interested in not only reading about the why and how of collaborative divorce, but also want a realistic view of what the process looks like, how it flows, and what its challenges are, this book is for you.

> **– James B. Morris, Jr., Ph.D., co-author of *Mindful Co-parenting: A Child-Friendly Path Through Divorce***

Joryn's ability to illustrate complicated legal processes by relaying her experiences in easy-to-read narrative stories is as impressive as ever in this new book. Readers will not only learn the differences between collaborative divorce and traditional courtroom divorce; they will feel the differences.

> **– Adam Cordover, J.D., collaborative lawyer and president of *Next Generation Divorce* Practice Group**

With her new book, *I Never Saw My Father Again*, Joryn Jenkins has contributed one more helpful tool in support of families seeking a peaceful resolution to their divorce-related disputes. Joryn has woven a lifetime of personal and professional stories into an engaging discussion about divorce, parenting, and the opportunity for finding collaborative solutions. You will enjoy reading this book — and you will be better off for it!

> **– Jeremy S. Gaies, Psy.D., co-author of *Mindful Co-parenting: A Child-Friendly Path Through Divorce***

This book is a must read . . . it puts all the pieces of the Collaborative Divorce together with realistic examples, leaving professionals with new insights, inspiration, and excitement about this process.

– Peggy Gummoe, LCSW, Collaborative Facilitator

Joryn has produced another fine 'guide' book for the challenging process of ending a marriage. She offers here a solid combination of information, self-questions, and stories of actual divorces that are in turn touching, shocking, relatable, and unimaginable. Anyone facing divorce will learn and experience within these pages how that process can be approached, either productively or not so much. May you read and choose a productive course.

– Carl Michael Rossi, JD, LPC, Former Board Member IACP, Founder and Executive Director of Collaborative Practice Professionals of Illinois

What They Said About Joryn's First Book,
War or Peace ...

"Joryn Jenkins' new book, War or Peace (Avoid the Destruction of Divorce Court), adds to the growing literature of Collaborative Divorce practice, a lively, client-centered guide focusing on the significant advantages of a collaborative team divorce — and the significant risks of choosing a less family-centric process for moving through the breakup and recovery process. While it is not meant to replace more comprehensive guides to the collaborative process or to the professional makeup of a full interdisciplinary collaborative team, the book speaks powerfully to clients at the emotional level – where divorce-related decisions are most often made – through vividly written accounts of how real people moving through divorce made good and not-so-good process choices, and where those choices led them. The particular power of this book lies in its rich narratives of the potential for grace and healing that collaborative practice offers to couples willing to embrace its tenets."

> **- Pauline Tesler, Co-Founder and first President, *International Academy of Collaborative Professionals*, and Director, *Integrative Law Institute at Commonweal***

"Joryn Jenkins has taken all of the mystery and confusion out of the divorce process and made it manageable and understandable for the client contemplating the end of a marriage. Most helpful are the examples she gives from her own experience as a respected 34-year lawyer and mediator. War or Peace should be on the shelf of every family lawyer. The book's description of the various roads to divorce is the most complete and accurate I have read and I plan to share it with all of my new clients. Thank you, Joryn, for your work as a peacemaker. This book is just the latest in a long line of contributions you have made to the practice of family law."

> **- Norma Trusch, Collaborative Lawyer, Former President of the *International Academy of Collaborative Professionals*, and Member, *Lone Star Collaborative Training***

"Oftimes someone facing divorce comes to it — based on recommendations from well-meaning friends, family, even professionals — with more than enough fear about what *might* happen if they are not excessive in their demands, aggressive in insisting they have 'rights' to some specific outcome, resistant to any concessions, and/or insistent upon punishment of the other person who's 'fault' it is that any of this is happening. In *War or Peace*, Joryn Jenkins has done a fine job of giving people insight into what *will* happen if they follow such a path, as well as how the collaborative practice process can support a divorcing couple in having discussions and reaching decisions that will actually meet their needs, and not just respond to their fears. Using general information, as well as a collection of tales that range from 'Dear God!' horrible to 'Aawww' heartwarming, Joryn has presented a volume here that anyone contemplating, facing, or going through a divorce should definitely read to get a valuable sense on how, and why, to avoid slash and burn warfare."

- carl Michael rossi, Collaborative Lawyer, *Collaborative Practice Chicago*, **Co-Editor,** *The World of Collaborative Practice*

"Anyone considering a divorce can certainly learn from [this] book how the divorce process works, in court and out of court, [and] how to best behave in order to achieve a maximum outcome. [Joryn's] examples of poor and inappropriate behavior and conduct, resulting in bad outcomes, were poignant. As a fellow experienced family law collaborative and cooperative lawyer, I was especially pleased with [her] descriptions and comments about how the collaborative law process works. [Her] passion and zeal in helping clients navigate the divorce process out of the risky, expensive, public and enhanced ill-will which emanates from litigation, is clearly articulated....

"With this book, Joryn has "advanced and elevated the practice of collaborative law, showing how [the courtless option] is the best choice for those persons who wish a non-combative divorce process."

- Sheldon E. Finman, Collaborative Lawyer, Member, *Collaborative Family Law Council of Florida*

"Sadly, I met Joryn years after my 'War Story' divorce. Had I known Joryn then, perhaps my children would have suffered less. Perhaps I would not have had to move out of town, away from my kids, and to put thousands of miles on my vehicle for weekend visitation. Perhaps I would have been there for their games and school functions. Defaulting to traditional courtroom divorce is an all-too-frequent story. But it doesn't have to be that way. Anyone considering divorce should read this book. With Joryn as the voice of the Collaborative Process, the peace of collaborative divorce should be our future."

- Gary Teaney, Father, CEO, *Transformational Consulting for Business*

"My courtroom divorce was initiated by a trial lawyer who failed to explain my options before we filed. Thus began eight years of destructive litigation, primarily because my father-in-law was a trial attorney, *and* a retired Army general. By the time Joryn got involved, it was too late. As Joryn explains in *War or Peace*, it was 'war from the get-go.' Although I 'won' at trial, I still suffered through years of hearings, appeals, and post-divorce motions, and incurred attorney's fees I'm still paying off.

"I wish this book had been available back then; I would have known to ask about collaborative divorce. I might have avoided the sometimes overwhelming stress and the huge financial burden of constant litigation. This book explains how everyone benefits from avoiding the traditional courtroom process of divorce. Although Joryn was always able to see the bigger picture and kept me on task, sharing parent responsibility in the best interests of our child, it was not easy in the face of the endless litigation. No one really 'wins' in court."

- Beth Hollis, Mother, Flight Attendant, Cancer Survivor

"Divorce feels like an anchor, threatening to drag you to the bottom of the sea. I was blessed to be offered alternatives to the traditional courtroom divorce. In this book, Joryn shares with everyone the courtless alternatives she explained to me so many years ago. Joryn took care of my parting from my husband of so many years with gentle conversations between us; she led us through diligent discussions to an amicable conclusion that we could both live with. She morphed my anchor into a sail so that we could both move on. Now, as a result of those diplomatic discussions, we are still friends, fifteen years later. And we had no children together! I can only hope that others will benefit from Joryn's guidance as I have done."

- Jan Powell, Former Wife, Writer, Editor

"I never wanted a divorce, but there came a time when it was inevitable. So I sought out an attorney who appreciated that I didn't want a war; I wanted to ensure that my son would still have a relationship with both of his parents after our divorce. In her book, *War or Peace*, Joryn explains what she shared with me, that *how* we divorce is a choice. Granted we both had to choose the same option or we'd end up in court, but at least we knew there *was* a choice. Once Joryn armed me with that information, she made it possible for me to sit down with my husband and arm him, as well. It was because of her schooling that we were able to get through the stress and pain of terminating our marriage without spending every penny we had on legal fees. Reading this book will do the same thing for you, if you, too, are bound for divorce."

- Charmaine Disimile, Mother, Administrative Assistant

"Don't trust just any lawyer to tell you the best way to get divorced. Trust Joryn; read her book. She makes sense!"

- Sam Sorbo, Author, Nationally Syndicated Radio Talk Show Host

Table of Contents

Foreword

There's an old saw that's very, very true: we "judges see good people at their worst in family court and bad people at their best in criminal court." Sadly, I know this from first-hand experience. I have been involved in our justice system for over 35 years as a police officer, attorney, and judge. Although I've tried nearly 1,500 cases, that number is dwarfed by those that went through the litigation process, including court hearings, and eventually settled before trial. During my decade on the Miami-Dade bench and then later on the nationally syndicated television show "Judge Alex," I presided over many cases in which litigation brought out the vindictive side of people. I repeatedly witnessed relationships and families that were completely shattered through litigious courtroom battles.

Family litigation, in particular, brings out the worst in people as they become intently focused on their positions and on defeating their soon to be ex-spouse, losing sight of everything else, including their children. Revenge and "winning" often become the goal in these courtroom battles, rather than seeking the best result for all involved. I've witnessed too many families destroyed by the hatred and vitriol spewed by one or both spouses who, after following a scorched Earth policy and expending every penny they had on attorney's fees in an effort to destroy their spouse, were left to sit back and watch their children grow up and treat or allow themselves to be treated the same way that Mommy and Daddy treated each other. That was their legacy.

In *I Never Saw My Father Again*, Joryn speaks directly to this issue. Written for the lay reader, her book is not the typical, dry, legal resource. It is both instructive and entertaining, filled with illustrative war stories drawn from years of experience in the courtroom, as well as tales of the peaceful results of the court-less alternative to traditional divorce litigation, the collaborative process. She explains how, instead of going to war, the clients move through the collaborative process with a support team comprised of their two lawyers and a facilitator, as well as a neutral financial professional. In the end, when successful (often estimated at over 90% of the time), they have negotiated a settlement agreeable to both of them. Thus, they "restructure" their family, rather than destroy it through the "win at all costs" mindset that the courtroom setting often creates.

Most importantly, instead of relying on a judge like me to say when each spouse will see their children and who will stay in the marital home, the clients are empowered to make these decisions themselves. As a result, the time-sharing schedules and the division of assets are tailored to suit the preferences and circumstances of the husband and wife, not the judge. Not that judges aren't good at what they do; we are. But we don't really know you or your kids, and we don't necessarily share your background, your ideals, your interests, your core beliefs, your history, or your values. In court, a judge decides the parties' assets, alimony, timesharing, child support – and everything else that matters – based on just a snapshot of the parties' life.

Just as importantly, by avoiding years of litigious courtroom battles, the spouses tend to save tremendous amounts of money and time by going the collaborative route. This leaves them with more money and assets to start the new chapter in their life, rather than having them give all of their savings to lawyers and create huge debts to fund the contentious litigation.

With over 30 years of litigation experience in both large and small law firms, and utilizing the perspective of a government lawyer as well as a law school professor, Joryn Jenkins uses her expertise to explore the complex issues raised and resolved in real collaborative divorce cases; recounting battles she fought in the family courtroom as well as peaceful resolutions she helped negotiate in the conference room. Having received one of the few awards conferred in the Supreme Court of the United States, for her ethics and professionalism, Joryn is the perfect messenger for this critical topic.

For these reasons, *I Never Saw My Father Again* is the ideal guide to help you learn about collaborative divorce and how it differs from traditional courtroom divorce. Once you are finished reading this book, you will be able to make an educated choice about how to approach your own divorce.

Personally, I suggest that you decide your own fate and collaborate.

Alex Ferrer, Host of the nationally syndicated court room TV Show *Judge Alex*, and 2008's Most Trustworthy Daytime TV Host
July 2015

Introduction

My books were due to arrive. The book launch was the next day and I'd placed the order late; after all, I'd had five proof copies delivered, but my four friends had only e-mailed me their mark ups the night before. I'd stayed up until 2:00 a.m., inputting their edits and then uploading the new text of *War or Peace* to my printer's website.

It would be close, but because the proofs had been delivered so quickly, I hoped, even at this last minute, that the copies would arrive in time for the launch.

Thank goodness it was a work day. A multitude of tasks distracted me as well as three consultations with potential clients. It wasn't until 3:30 that I realized that the postman had delivered the mail and I asked Alex if I'd received a package. I had.

Per his normal routine, he'd walked it to the back door of the office, which has easy access to my parking spot in the alley just outside. "Yes, there's a box. I put it by the back door."

He must have forgotten that I was expecting . . . waiting for . . . well, really, *hoping* for my books. It wasn't *his* baby, after all.

I literally ran to open it. There sat the loveliest cardboard box I had ever seen, even bigger than I had expected. A hundred books *would* take up a lot of space, wouldn't it? Still, I expected it to be awfully heavy.

I tentatively attempted to lift it. Hhmm. Not *so* heavy, after all. But they *were* just paperbacks, right?

When I hoisted it, I could barely see over the top. I carried it into the kitchen and placed it on the table. Grabbing a knife out of the utensil drawer, I sliced through the tape.

By this time, a crowd had gathered. Sheila and Lori had remembered that I was hoping the delivery would make it in time. I didn't want to be the only author out of eleven without books for the *Collaboration Book Launch.*

The promotion had been planned for months, and while we'd each struggled to finish on time, fifteen of us hadn't made the deadline. Our launch date had been set far in advance, a goal carved in stone, to push us to complete our writing projects.

Nevertheless, as my mother had always told me, "Hope for the best; plan for the worst." The week before the launch, I'd contacted the graphic artist who'd designed the cover and got pre-order forms and high-quality bookmarks. That way, I'd at least have *something* to hand out to our guests if the books didn't arrive.

One side of the bookmark was a replica of the book's cover with information about the website where it would be available for order. The other included a quote from a national radio talk show host, about how compelling her read of the book had been. (I'd sent her a PDF of *War or Peace* a few weeks earlier. She had graciously skimmed it and provided her two cents in the form of a book review that would also appear on the back cover.)

I grasped the panels of the cardboard box and pulled them open. Inside, piled tightly, lay . . . two stacks of baby diapers. No wonder it hadn't been heavy. Sheila and Lori peeked over my shoulders and burst out laughing. I snapped the panels closed and, smiling regretfully, heaved a sigh of disappointment.

The book launch was an amazing celebration. In addition to the pre-order forms and the bookmarks, I displayed my banners and my five marked up proofs, for "show and tell." At least folks could see what the book would look like. Many of the guests paid for copies of the book in advance.

When it came time for me to speak, I differentiated myself from the rest of the pack; "I'm the only author here who has no books!" Everyone thought it was funny.

I wasn't there to sell books anyway; I was there to spread the word about the collaborative process as an option for obtaining a good divorce, a kinder, gentler divorce. And that's what I talked about during my remarks. As a result, several guests asked for my business card.

Arguably, the most important component of the collaborative divorce process is the planning by the professionals, a crucial element to every stages of the process. Why? Because "a stitch in time saves nine," and all that. Something *always* goes awry in a process dependent on human emotion fraught with grief and anger. A good collaborative team consistently plans in minute detail every aspect of the work. That way, we minimize the number of surprises, as well as the impact of any one unexpected event.

In this volume, my second book about the collaborative divorce process,[1] I explore the more challenging issues that can arise in a collaborative setting. In addition, I offer accounts showing how those issues were resolved in real cases in remarkably short order by good teamwork. In contrast, I describe some of the more difficult cases that I've tried in divorce court, and what happened thereafter.

I hope you benefit from my experiences, enjoy the stories, and find value in their similarities and contrasts. Feel free to contact me with tales of your own experiences, whether you are a collaborative professional, or a person who has been through a divorce of any kind, dissolution of a partnership, or your employment, or a corporate relationship, or, of course, your marriage, at Joryn@OpenPalmLaw.com.

And if you want to know more, you can always check out our website at http://OpenPalmLaw.com/ and my blog at http://OpenPalmLaw.com/blog/.

---

[1] The first, *War or Peace, Avoid the Destruction of Divorce Court*, is an introduction to and discusses the basic concepts behind the collaborative divorce protocol. It is available on Amazon (http://amzn.to/1uPmzbq), as well as on the *Open Palm* website (http://www.openpalmlaw.com/WarOrPeace). The e-books are sold at Barnes & Noble for your Nook at http://bit.ly/1sGwg7i; by Kobo for your Kindle at http://bit.ly/1AAD8rC; and by iBooks for your Mac at http://bit.ly/1z3EtF0.

Chapter One

Families Don't Belong in the Courtroom

Divorce is one of the most stressful life events that a person can experience, being both extremely emotional, and, generally, expensive. Even the most amicable divorces wound families, not only the two people divorcing, but their children, their parents, their siblings, and their close friends. Individuals, including children, are often forced to pick sides in a war not of their own making.

Traditional courtroom divorces pit spouses against one another in an adversarial setting designating them as "opposing parties." Even if they try to avoid a war, once they retain attorneys, the battle usually begins. Trial attorneys are trained to make the road as bumpy as possible for the opposing party. They seek out the worst parts of a person, bring those traits to everyone's attention, and then magnify them.

But when it comes to families, is this really the best idea? Our clients aren't criminals, or people involved in a civil dispute whose relationship ends once the complaint is filed. We're dealing with families who will be forced, by the nature of their relationships, to spend time with one another indefinitely as their children grow, graduate, wed, and have babies themselves.

Children are generally the most helpless victims in the adversarial process. While they're trying to cope with the fact that Mommy and Daddy don't live together any longer, and that they can't sleep in a house where both of them are in the next room, children are often thrown into the middle of the divorce war.

1

Parents seek parenting and timesharing evaluations. In these, mental health professionals often called ""evaluators" delve into every aspect of the family to determine which spouse should "win" more time with their children.

In some cases, the parties file domestic violence injunctions to get the upper hand in the courtroom battle. Such court conflicts often result in the children not seeing one of their parents for extended periods of time. They can result in exchanging the children at police stations, where it's difficult for the kids to feel like the back and forth time between the parents is normal or positive. Sometimes, children are even permitted to testify, forced to choose sides and to tell the judge which parent they love more. They take that memory, that *betrayal* into their adulthood.

Costs skyrocket. Money from the spouses' savings, funds that should be used for their children's college funds, and reserves from their own parents' retirement funds are thrown away on attorney's fees, experts' fees, and other litigation costs. Family assets dwindle, and parties end up fighting over who will be responsible for the debt, rather than who will receive the assets.

Health suffers from the trauma of living in a constant state of stress and fear of the unknown, not knowing what's going to happen in your personal life. The detrimental effects of a lengthy divorce may plague people for years afterward, and possibly for a lifetime.

But there *is* a better way. Any process outside of court is better, of course. But the holistic approach of the collaborative process is constructive, not destructive, as is the litigation process. The professional team considers the entire family and aims for a resolution where everyone wins, rather than just one person or, worse, no one. It doesn't involve the courts in an adversarial way or rely on court-imposed resolutions.

Instead, the process permits the clients to negotiate in an atmosphere of honesty, cooperation, integrity, and professionalism geared toward the future well-being of the restructured family. Each client hires an attorney trained in collaborative practice and in interest-based negotiation. The attorneys will withdraw and trial attorneys must be retained if the collaborative process fails and any adversarial proceedings are initiated. This assures that everyone, including the lawyers, is committed to the settlement process.

The team includes mental health professionals, either one who acts as a neutral facilitator who guides the meetings, or two who work as coaches for the clients. Either way, they are trained at spotting emotional pitfalls that may keep the parties from effectively negotiating. They also assist the clients in developing their parenting plan.

In addition, the team has a neutral financial professional who often guides the meetings. This member helps the clients compile their financial discovery documents and provides ideas for settlement of their financial matters.

Each collaborative professional focuses on his or her strengths and trainings to help the parties in the most effective and cost-efficient way possible. These divorces generally take much less time and cost much less money than traditional litigated ones. Clients are usually able to maintain their relationships with one another and to learn communication and interaction skills that will help them in their lives *after* their divorce. And this, of course, protects their relationships with all of those around them, both in their immediate family and outside of it.

I Never Saw My Father Again

Did my book title catch your eye? Are you one of the many, many children of divorce? Did you look through the table of contents and turn to this chapter first?

I often lecture about the horrors of traditional courtroom divorce and compare its negative effects to the positive aspects of cooperative and collaborative divorce. I always tell the story of how my parents were divorced when I was seven years old. "My mother loaded us kids into the van and moved us 3000 miles away. . . and I never saw my father again."

Every time I tell that story, dead silence follows. Shock waves reverberate. People don't know what to say although I can see them immediately trying to gauge my age. (I'm 58 now.) Of course, they feel sorry for me. I can tell that they're thinking. "It's such a horrible thing to happen to a small child." "Oh, and there were several kids, not just one." Some folks even think about my dad. "Why did *she* do that?" "What could *he* possibly have done to deserve it?"

I have no idea why people assume that my story is an outlier. It's not so unusual. I was at breakfast the other day with six gentlemen from my referral networking group, from all walks of life. We began discussing our backgrounds and I told this story. After all, it defines who I am and why I do what I do for a living. But two others told variations on the same theme. Consider that; three out of seven, nearly half of us, had the same story!

Andrew was born in England. His father kidnapped him when he was seven and relocated to another country. His mother couldn't find him for several months. When she did, she recovered him, and he never saw his father again.

Gary grew up in the Midwest. He was abducted by his father when he was six and he never saw his mother again.

I was first kidnapped by my father when I was six, when my parents were separated, just before they divorced. He only took me to another city for three days, and returned me at the end of the weekend. I remember clearly how distraught my mother was. Yet she turned around and kidnapped all of us, my three sisters and me, once the divorce was official.

Last October, I went to lunch in Washington, D.C. with a group of . . . well, let's just say that I was the youngest person there. We were all lawyers with our spouses, and we'd all been very active in the American Inns of Court movement 15-20 years earlier. There were 22 of us seated around the table. We circled the conversation around the table, bringing everyone up to speed on our last 15 years. (It had been that long since we'd all been at one event together.)

One women, probably 68 or 70, told the story of her parents' divorce. The divorce wasn't recent event, but her reunion with her 91-year-old dad was. She hadn't seen him for over 50 years, but, when her mother died, she saw the opportunity to reconnect.

He wasn't at all what she had expected and was thrilled when she reached out. What was so telling to me was the elation she shared with all of us, the delight of having her father in her life once again. Something she had never dreamed possible while her mother was alive.

I always tell my story in terms of . . . I never saw my father again. But the other side of that coin, of course, is that he never saw any of his four daughters again. I'll never know why, whether he chose not to seek us out, or my mother made it clear that he'd never be welcome, and he just accepted her decision.

She used to tell us that he never paid any child support, despite that he was a doctor making loads of money. But then again, when I was 19 years old, he called me out of the blue. We talked briefly. I was away at college but I, of course, having only one parent upon whom I was totally emotionally dependent, was a mama's girl. So I reported back to her and asked her why she thought he had called because he hadn't said. She suggested that he was calling to find out if I was emancipated so that he didn't have to pay child support anymore.

What?

So which was it? Did he pay child support or not? And did he actually call, hoping to reestablish contact?

There's no question that children become pawns in many divorces or that they're injured when they're used that way. The collaborative restructuring process is a better alternative for not only for the adults, but also the children, than the emotional and psychological devastation that is inevitable in the traditional courtroom divorce process.

Folks seeking to dissolve their marriages aren't the only ones caught up in an overburdened and overwhelming judicial system. Anyone seeking to enforce his rights can find himself unexpectedly ensnared in litigation, appealing to someone he doesn't know, a judge, to ensure that he receives his due, whether it's medical expenses from a slip and fall, or fair timesharing arrangements with his child. However, any dispute that can be brought before a court in a lawsuit can also be addressed in other ways, in mediation or in the collaborative dispute resolution process, for example. It just takes both disputants to agree to handle it outside the courtroom. That's what finally happened here, although only after too much money had been spent and too much damage had been done to the relationship between the parents involved.

The Parent

David was adorable. He was blond-haired, blue-eyed, and six feet tall, a twenty-eight-year-old firefighter built like Adonis. He came to my office in jeans, a t-shirt, and clever leather sandals. He had just discovered that his erstwhile girlfriend, Jamie, a deputy sheriff, was expecting. He'd apparently impregnated her during their failed attempt to patch up their broken relationship. He wanted advice.

His first tentative question was fairly generic. "How much time am I allowed to spend with our child?"

"How much time do you want?"

He laughed, nervously. "As much as I'm allowed. But Jamie says that I can only see him or her every other weekend."

He was clearly unaware that his rights as a father should be the same as the mother's, all other things being equal. "Do you have any other children?"

"No, although Jamie has a three-year-old daughter from before we got together. I spent a lot of time with her while we were dating. She's a cute kid and doesn't get to see her father very much."

I ignored that loaded comment for the time being. "Are you looking forward to becoming a dad?"

"Oh, my gosh, yes, I'm very excited! But Jaime isn't really speaking to me since we broke up. I found out that she was pregnant from another deputy I know, so I called her to find out what was going on. When I asked whether she would allow me to spend time with our child, she told me that I didn't know how to be a parent and that it would depend on how things went."

I frowned, not focusing on his unconscious need to ask for her permission, rather than to request what was arguably his right. "What's that supposed to mean?"

He smiled, a rueful expression weighing down his features. "I think she was trying to insinuate that we should get back together. But that didn't work out very well the first time, or the second."

Then I said the smartest thing I'd said in a long time, weighing my words carefully. "You know, everyone has to be a parent for the first time."

He stared at me. I could almost see the light bulb go on. "Yes. I guess I knew that. I just never thought of it that way."

We talked for a little while about all those pregnancy books that women tend to buy when they discover they're expecting. You see them all the time offered at garage sales. And there are many books about raising a child, *The First Year*, *The Second Year*, and so forth and so on. I suggested that he get some of those to better educate himself.

I asked about his childhood. Because his father had recently passed away, he'd gone back home out of concern about his mother living alone. She'd moved into the mother-in-law apartment on the property. Because they were very close, I suggested that he talk with her about what it was like raising him. He agreed.

Soon after he returned with a signed retainer agreement and his mother. She was tiny but vivacious, a bubbling 50-year-old woman with lots of energy, excited about the prospect of welcoming her first grandchild into the world. She paid my retainer fee, and we three chatted about how David should approach his ex-girlfriend about taking an active part in parenting their child. He'd already suggested a collaborative approach to her, but she stated authoritatively that he couldn't force her to do anything. Ultimately, we agreed that he'd have to file a petition to establish paternity. She wasn't resistant to communicating in the first place, and reluctant to discuss his role in their child's life.

During the ensuing months, he stopped by frequently, although it was always a brief visit. We talked often about how to establish a co-parenting relationship. She wouldn't even discuss her delivery options with him, and certainly hadn't invited him to be present. He did learn that he'd be the proud father of a little girl.

In the meantime, our litigation dance commenced. Her lawyer, a friend of mine, answered our petition in a fairly non-contentious manner. I filed a very non-confrontational request for the judge to order us to mediation. After all, the only issues to be resolved were timesharing and child support, and the latter wasn't even an issue once the parents' salaries had been quantified. One simply computed the statutory amount due from one to the other depending on how many overnights each parent was to enjoy with their daughter.

Timesharing would be both more difficult, and possibly easier than with two average parents who have weekday, 9-to-5 jobs. In such cases, both parents compete for the same quality free time. But both firefighters and sheriff's deputies work shifts, and the shifts alternate periodically. The good news for David and for Jamie was that both the sheriff's office and the city were agreeable to working out complementary shifts for them. This would "expand the pie," and also make it possible that their daughter was almost never in daycare, but always with one of her parents, or with her paternal grandmother.

Nevertheless, whenever he approached her, she was very

difficult, unwilling to discuss sharing time with "my daughter." Word came from her lawyer that she was planning to breast-feed; this would allegedly require my client to visit with their daughter for only an hour or two at a time. In fact, Jamie was only offering him timesharing if he exercised it in her home.

A transparent ploy, I thought.

We resolved nothing during informal negotiations, try as I might. She was near term before we were able to schedule a mediation that both lawyers, the mediator, and the two clients were able to attend. It would take place a month *after* the baby was due.

The fateful day arrived. My office is centrally located, so Kendall, Jamie's lawyer, agreed to mediate in my conference room. Participants trickled in one at a time, except that Jamie brought Amie, the baby whom she had named without any input from David. Jamie was a pretty, dark-haired lady, muscular and of average height. She placed the infant's carrier in the middle of my conference room table. Amie slept soundly while we talked.

On my advice, David had asked his mother to stay home.

He'd petitioned for paternity so it was up to us to commence negotiations. The mediator invited me to make my opening statement.

It was important for Jamie to know why David should have equal timesharing. He had kept me up to speed on her arguments to him in person, so I addressed those first. I *couldn't* tell her that the law in Florida *required* equal timesharing because the legislature hadn't yet passed that statute; that's still to come. But I *could* explain why our judges were already starting each final evidentiary hearing with the idea firmly planted that both parents were entitled to equal time with their children.

Jamie had told David that he was a narcissist and only wanted equal timesharing in order to eliminate the child support he would otherwise have to pay. Other women who have been primary caregivers during the marriage have also explained to me (or to the judge) that their husbands were asking for 50/50 timesharing as a control tactic, or to harass them, or to try to turn the children against them.

While I'm certain that there are situations in which these

concerns are right on target, in my experience, most of time, this isn't the case.

I commenced in generalities, to make it easier for her to acknowledge the truth of what I wanted her to hear. "Although the trend is away from this custom, more often than not, in most of my divorce cases, moms have been the primary care providers for the children. Dads, on the other hand, have been more involved with their careers and supporting their families, even when both parents have jobs outside the home. I'm guessing that this has been true with respect to your relationship with the father of your older daughter, am I right?"

She nodded. "He sees her on alternating weekends."

"In an intact family, when the parents are still together, the mother keeps Dad's image alive and well in the kid's minds while he's at work. In addition, he's helped by the fact that his footprint is all over the home, reminders that he's intimately involved in the family. His shoes are by the front door, his family photos are on the walls, his shaving kit is in the bathroom, his sports gear is in the garage, and his clothes are hanging in the closet." I caught her eye again. "Am I right?"

She nodded again.

"Post separation, that changes. Physical reminders of Dad are removed from Mom's home. The likelihood that she'll make any effort to keep him alive in the kids' minds is also greatly reduced, especially when the break-up is hostile."

I paused, waiting for someone to interrupt. No one did. "Now Dad has to carry the weight of his relationship with his children by himself. Mom no longer helps and she may do the reverse. If the children still spend a disproportionate amount of time residing with their mother rather than with Dad, when she enters a new romantic relationship, the kids will be spend more time with her new boyfriend than they do with him."

Still, no one said a word. "Now Dad must be concerned about protecting his place in the lives of his children." I switched gears. "I understand that David was something of a father figure to your toddler while you were dating. I'm sure that caused some friction between you and her birth father." David and I had discussed this and I knew it to be true. Her nod was almost imperceptible.

"Just because you and he aren't involved anymore doesn't mean he doesn't want to be Amie's dad." My words were hitting home. "Let's see if we can work this out so that she has the best of both worlds, the one her mother can give her, as well as the one her father has to offer."

After opening statements, we broke into separate caucus rooms. The mediator, an older attorney who had restricted her practice to mediating years ago, spent two hours with Jamie and her lawyer before coming in to see us. While we waited, we discussed our options and why they were taking so long. I assured David that this wasn't a sign of difficulty; I'd chosen our mediator well.

She entered the room with a smile. "Good opening, even though you started at a disadvantage because of the situation with her first daughter. You gave her a lot to think about and apparently Kendall's been working on her since she retained him. You guys laid the foundation for me pretty well."

"Does she understand that the judge will start with the idea that 50/50 makes sense for most families? The burden will be on her to show why David *shouldn't* get 50/50?"

"She seems to get it. She's not stupid, just hard-headed. And, luckily for us, David hasn't been pressuring her, or pushing her buttons while he waited for this mediation."

"Have they made a timesharing offer?"

She laid it out for us. "They've proposed a plan that gives him 40% of the overnights, but I think if we go back with a 50/50 plan that maximizes both parties' time, I can get her to accept that. It's not about the child support for her."

David interjected, "I can pay her some child support if she needs that. She's got two kids now, and Milly's dad doesn't always pay his on time."

"That's probably not necessary," the mediator said, "although you can always give her extra money later if she needs it."

I added, "David, don't get yourself locked into a payment that the law doesn't require."

So we proposed the timesharing plan that we'd walked in with. And that's the plan with which we walked out two hours later.

Amie is three years old now. David occasionally forwards cell phone photos of himself and his beautiful daughter from Disney World, where she's riding on his shoulders, or the pool, where he's teaching her to swim, or the living room floor, where she's making words with those brightly colored plastic fridge letter magnets. Of course, she's always grinning, and she has the same exact grin as her dad. Here's the last e-mail missive I received from him:

Dear Ms. Jenkins,

Aug 29th Amie celebrated her 3rd birthday. We celebrated with a trip to the beach. It also reminded me of what a different time it was three years ago, and made me thankful for all the help I received from you and your staff back then. Amie and I spend a lot of time together. In fact, her mother's schedule has changed, so she now spends five days a week with me. (Some weeks more!) She talks a lot these days, and likes quoting characters from her favorite movie "Cars." I've been building a tree house for her (it's never too soon for a tree house), and she loves taking her "toolbox" from Grandma up with me so she can help, too. Her favorite place to go is Lowry Park, and she likes calling to the monkeys and riding the merry-go-round every time we go. She's known as "Peeps" by all of my family and friends.

I want you to know how much I appreciate all the work you did and patience you had for me and my case. I want you, Lori, Sheila, and the rest of your staff to know you have been a big part in the time I now get to spend with my daughter.

Thank you,

Your grateful client, David Goodman

My clients often hear me say "every parent's a parent for the first time." But not everyone *should* be a parent. Although many of my clients have entered my offices with every intention of cutting the other parents out of, not only their own lives, but also the lives of their children, I'm usually successful in softening and then altering that self-centered perspective. Only rarely have I absolutely agreed that a parent really had no business being a parent. This was one of those times.

The Clothes Dryer

Not everyone is cut out to be a parent. Sometimes a client's story makes me wonder what he or she (or, usually, his or her spouse) was thinking. Pamela Jones came to us for her divorce from Tom when she realized his mental wellbeing was in question. She was especially concerned about his lack of sensible caregiving skills regarding their children.

Often a prospective client will insist that his or her spouse is mentally ill. We point out that if her husband or his wife is psychotic, what does that say about our client, who has lived with him or her for years? This perspective helps bring our client to the table ready for a fair resolution.

This case was a little different.

Pamela Jones was a pretty ash blond, no more than 5'2" tall, who wore her hair in what we used to call a "page boy." She was in her mid-thirties, and had married a man ten years her senior a decade earlier. They had boys, eight and three, and a daughter in between, six years old.

One Sunday afternoon following a nap, Pamela couldn't find Teddy, their three-year-old. The older two children were playing quietly in their bedrooms, but he was absent, and the older kids had no idea where he was. With increasing concern she searched the house. She found her husband alone in the den, drinking a beer, eating chips, and watching a football game.

"Tom, where's Teddy? I can't find him anywhere!"

Tom responded calmly, without taking his eyes off the television screen. "I put him in the dryer,"

"What? The dryer?" Perhaps she had misunderstood him.

He explained, as though it was the most natural thing in the world, "He was upset and wouldn't take his nap, so I put him to sleep in the clothes dryer."

She was flabbergasted. As she rushed to the laundry room, she called over her shoulder. "How long has he been in there?"

Tom responded matter-of-factly, "Probably about forty minutes or so."

Both the dryer door and the laundry room door were completely closed. When she removed Teddy from the dryer, his face was bright red, his clothing was soaked in sweat, and he appeared groggy and sluggish.

When she returned with the toddler to the den, Tom showed no concern for his well-being, much less any remorse. He acted like putting the child to sleep in the dryer was standard operating procedure.

She took Teddy to his regular pediatrician that day, just to check him out after the ordeal. Later, at the insistence of her own therapist and Teddy's doctor, she reported the incident to the child abuse hotline.

As it turned out, she was already seeing a marriage counselor. She'd invited Tom to participate but, when he refused, she continued on her own.

He'd recently begun exhibiting strange obsessive behavior towards her by e-mailing her numerous times a day. In addition, he insisted she provide him with a detailed schedule of every place she was going and the timeframe in which she would be there.

Until recently, they had enjoyed a traditional marriage in which he worked as the primary breadwinner and she functioned as the primary caregiver. After she petitioned for divorce they continued to live together. This made her very uncomfortable because there weren't enough bedrooms for them to sleep separately. Eventually, she was granted exclusive use and possession of the home. The judge ordered him to move out, "kicking and screaming," as it were.

Pamela had suggested that they speak to the children together about the change in their living situation, and Tom had seemed to agree. Upon leaving, however, he had made a scene in front of the children. While she was inside tidying and packing for him, he apparently interrupted their playing in the front yard to announce that he was moving out.

After he left, she discovered all three kids weeping hysterically. Between his hiccupping sobs, Teddy shrieked, "Papa says you want him to leave! Papa wants us to stay together but not you. What would Jesus do? He would forgive! You need to forgive Papa!"

Tom's inappropriate communications continued. After he returned the children from dinner one night, Teddy informed her that he'd told the children that he only had $7.00 in his bank account. Her daughter explained, "He said he didn't have any money, and it's all your fault." The children told her that their grandmother was helping Papa because she wouldn't.

The following day, the school counselor called her. She told Pamela that her daughter had told her that her papa had to sleep in his car.

Tom's comments to the children were not only completely inappropriate, but also confused them. His words violated both the standing order entered in the case and the general principles of shared parenting. Obviously, the children became concerned when they realized that something was going on in the home. However, his discussions were designed to damage their relationship with Pamela and portray her as the "bad guy." This selfish behavior harmed their mental and emotional well-being and was counter-productive to co-parenting.

When she finally petitioned to dissolve their marriage, he

stopped putting money into their joint bank account. This forced Pamela to charge groceries, the children's pharmacy, and school expenses to her personal credit card. But he also had access to the card. He used it to purchase, among other things, Yoga classes and new bed sheets. All the while he insisted there wasn't enough money in their joint account to cover all the marital bills, although there had always been enough *before* she filed for divorce.

When he was still living with her, he refused to perform any home maintenance. One weekend, after he left under court order, he used a screwdriver to gain access and removed a ladder from inside. When she questioned him, he admitted to breaking in and said only that "he needed the ladder for something."

Although she ensured that the children called him every day, often several times, he telephoned them so often it distracted and upset them. When they were unavailable, he called repeatedly and left voice messages. One night, he called five times in one hour which filled Pamela's mailbox. If there had been an emergency, she and the children would have been unreachable. While she wanted him to have a close relationship with his children, these calls were designed to harass her.

The Joneses eventually agreed on a settlement which gave Pamela the majority of the timesharing. Afterwards, she grew increasingly concerned about Teddy's mental health because he began exhibiting behavior similar to Tom's. She was afraid that he had inherited the same inclinations. She repeatedly asked Tom to agree to allow Teddy to go to counseling, but he fought every attempt. She had to move for an order to get Teddy help.

After the divorce, Tom's excessive calls and texts continued. He told the children that they shouldn't call Pamela when they were in his care because she would "put him in jail" or "make sure that the police took him away." This made the children anxious, hindered his relationship with them, and was clearly detrimental. Additionally, he often left them home alone for more than two hours, extended times by themselves which frightened them. He also failed to get them to school on time.

He never seemed concerned with their overall well-being. While his behavior wasn't usually horrendous enough to warrant supervised timesharing, it was selfish and harmful.

In contrast, Pamela was a very loving caregiver, and by having them most of the time, was able to make them feel safe and secure. As years passed after the divorce, he stepped back and allowed her to have an even more prominent role in the children's lives. Even though this came from selfish reasons, he had finally acted in the children's best interest.

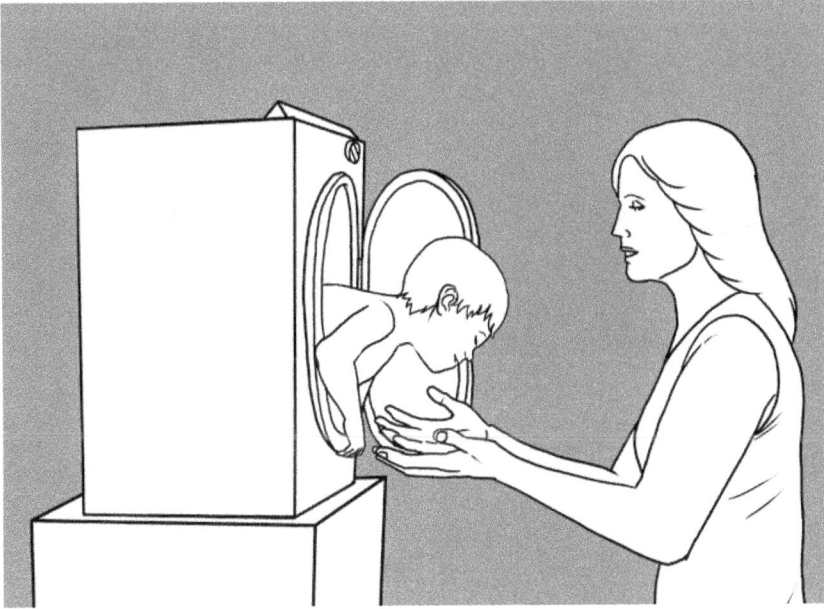

Chapter Two

The Disclosure Statement

If you choose to participate in the collaborative process, you and your spouse or partner would each have an attorney and a shared commitment to avoid litigation. The process involves informal discussions and joint meetings in order to settle issues where the participants agree to be honest and mutually respectful. Both clients and their counsel commit to resolving differences without resorting to court proceedings. This process utilizes informal exchanges of financial and possibly other information and may involve jointly engaged neutral professionals. Both clients are assigned tasks to assist in the process. Parenting plans, allocating parental responsibilities and parenting time with children, are jointly worked out by parents with the goal of serving the best interests of the family as a whole. The clients use their best efforts to arrive at solutions that address their fundamental interests (needs, values, concerns, and priorities) in order to reach an acceptable settlement. If the matter cannot settle through the collaborative process, the collaborative lawyers must withdraw.

What to Consider When Deciding Whether
to Participate in the Collaborative Process

The following may be advantages of the collaborative process:

✓ Collaborative practice contemplates a series of meetings to gather information, to develop and evaluate options, and to allow each party time to make informed decisions. During these meetings, the clients will have the comfort of professional advice and guidance from their respective collaborative lawyers.

✓ The collaborative process preserves privacy by not airing differences in a public forum. Most settlement terms and financial disclosures can be kept from the public record.

✓ The clients retain control over the outcome. Collaborative settlements are more sustainable over time and invite more consistent compliance than do court-ordered mandates.

✓ The collaborative process helps parents develop and preserve a cooperative relationship that will benefit their children as they co-parent.

✓ The inevitable increase in hostility and conflict that results from adversarial litigation emotionally damages litigants' children. The collaborative process is designed to minimize conflict, both during the divorce and after.

✓ Extended family relationships and friendships are more likely to be preserved in the collaborative process.

✓ The collaborative process levels the playing field by ensuring that all fees are paid from marital funds or otherwise allocated in an acceptable manner.

✓ The collaborative process requires the professionals and the clients to explore options that address the interests of both clients and their child(ren), rather than to take tactical positions to obtain an advantage.

✓ The collaborative process encourages creative solutions to meet the clients' needs, which may differ from what the court would decide.

✓ Everyone has an economic incentive to work toward settlement – the clients because of the high cost of litigation and the lawyers because they will be required to withdraw if settlement cannot be achieved.

✓ The collaborative process is confidential. Litigation is public.

✓ The team approach is one of the major benefits of the collaborative process. The process allows the clients to jointly engage neutral professionals to help them resolve their differences and improve their communication.

The following could be disadvantages of the collaborative process:

✓ You can't get your "day in court" in the collaborative process. (Of course, you don't usually get your "day in court" in litigation either. Most litigated cases settle before trial.)

✓ If the matter is not resolved and litigation counsel is retained, there may be some duplication of effort as the second lawyer catches up.

✓ Should trial be necessary, trial preparation will have been delayed and important evidence may be unavailable.

✓ Court-ordered mechanisms to compel production of information are not available.

✓ Emergency, pre-emptive relief (e.g. a restraining order) regarding property and children may not be available.

✓ Neutral experts retained during the collaborative process may not be allowed to participate if the case does not settle. You might need to hire and pay for additional experts to support your position in court.

The following are other concerns relating to the collaborative process:

✓ The collaborative process is not appropriate when punitive action is sought, such as contempt proceedings to enforce prior orders.

✓ The collaborative process may not be appropriate if an acceptable level of trust is lacking.

✓ The collaborative process prohibits taking tactical advantage of another's mistakes, oversights, and misinformation. Litigation sometimes allows the litigant with the less meritorious case to prevail.

✓ Protective orders in family violence cases are not obtained in the collaborative process.

✓ The collaborative process is not suitable if a party feels threatened, intimidated, or in an unequal bargaining position, even with the assistance of counsel.

✓ No one who feels coerced into participating in the collaborative process should agree to it.

✓ If the clients feel compelled to vindicate and defend themselves from accusations of wrong-doing or to expose the wrong-doing of another, the privacy of the collaborative process may not be satisfying.

✓ If the dispute requires the judicial determination of a preliminary question of law or fact upon which all the negotiations depend, the collaborative process may be premature.

✓ The collaborative process contemplates the collaborative professional team's ability to communicate confidentially without informing or copying the clients so that the team can work together to attain the goal of reaching an acceptable settlement.

✓ If a party desires to conceal certain information that could affect the outcome of the case, the collaborative process is inappropriate. The clients are required to share all relevant information and documents in the collaborative process. Concealment is not tolerated. In litigation, if properly requested, all relevant information must be disclosed as well.

✓ It is ultimately your decision whether or not to engage in the collaborative process.

Speaking in front of an audience, to a decision maker, whether a judge or a jury, is very scary. We trial lawyers do it every day; it's a necessary component of the profession we've chosen, and therefore, we take it for granted. It's *not* so easy for our clients, and this is yet another reason that a collaborative process is preferable for them, but most lawyers tend to forget or ignore the stress that litigation can cause the average guy. Or gal.

I do *not*.

The Best & Hardest Question

I was 10 years old in 1967, and, courtesy of my grandfather, I owned five shares of *Technical Tape Incorporated*. All five of us, my younger sisters and my 31-year-old mother, were living with my grandparents back then, in New Rochelle, New York. This was *maybe* an hour outside of New York City. When notice of the annual shareholders' meeting arrived, I was very excited to receive mail addressed to me.

I informed my mother that I wanted to attend.

She didn't make fun of me. Instead, she asked what I hoped to accomplish by attending. I have no idea what I told her, but, after what was apparently an insightful discussion, she agreed. She gave me permission to skip school, and helped me with the itinerary. Because she'd be at work elsewhere in the City, she also gave me directions to find her if I got lost, and money for cab fare.

(Remember: no cell phones back then!)

Her belief was that the trip would be good for me, educational. She doubted I'd be bold enough to say anything to anyone while I was there.

That morning, I chose my favorite Polly Flinders dress, a bright turquoise with a yellow-and-pink smocked breast. Before leaving for work, my mother gave me hand written travel instructions, which I tucked carefully into my purse, along with the necessary money. Later, my grandmother drove me to catch the train in our old VW bus.

At the station, I bought my roundtrip ticket and boarded the one for New York City. Although I had brought a book to read, I spent the journey staring out the window. My heart pounded so hard I could hear my pulse in my head. I wondered what surprises lay in wait.

An hour later, without the security of an adult hand to grasp, I stepped into the disorienting cavern that was Grand Central Station. My mission led me to the information booth, an island of assistance in the middle of the main atrium. Adults surged around me in that massive arena which seemed as large as an airport hangar.

Once pointed in the right direction, I found the tunnel to the correct subway line. After I purchased two tokens, one for leaving and one for returning, I found the proper train line. At Fifth Avenue, I alighted and eventually discovered the exit where passengers streamed onto the street of my destination.

Bright May sunshine enveloped me at the head of the stairs. At first, I headed the wrong way. After a pause to orient myself, I changed direction and, in due course, found the building. After I arrived at the correct floor, I located the conference room. Through the double-door entry, two hundred middle-aged men in black suits, starched white button-down oxfords, and unimaginative neckties milled around, talking and exchanging business cards until instructed to take their seats.

I signed in at the registration table out front. I stuck my name badge to my breast. My mother had prepped me for this; I sat in the front row. The meeting commenced.

Although I don't remember much about the beginning, I

vividly recall wondering why the chairman of the board kept using the word "fluctuate" during his speech on "The State of the Corporation." I'd never heard nor read the word before. So, when he finally called for questions, my hand shot into the air. Unruffled, he called on me immediately. I stood. "What does the word fluctuate mean?"

He smiled while the sea of men around me chuckled. "Why, that's a marvelous question! Fluctuate is the word I'm using to describe the large swings in value of *Technical Tape* stock this year, when the price goes way up and then way down, and then way up again. Does that answer your question, young lady?"

"Yes, sir, it does. Thank you." I sat again, quite pleased with myself. Now I had a story to tell.

At the end of the meeting, I returned to New Rochelle, called my grandmother from the pay phone at the station, and waited for her to pick me up. That evening, my family congratulated me on my exciting undertaking. My mother wanted to know every detail, so I happily recounted the events of the day.

My grandmother asked for more particulars while she was making dinner the next day, and so I reveled in narrating the story again. When Saturday night arrived for my grandparents' weekly bridge game, my grandfather called me into the living room and invited me to tell our guests about my trip into the City. For several days, I enjoyed a small measure of fame in our household.

Then . . . the Box arrived. It was fairly large, almost half my height, but also oddly light. I lifted it easily. A mystery. It was addressed to me with a New York City return address. Everyone wanted to know what was in it, and the entire family gathered round.

It was securely wrapped in tape. My grandfather handed me his Swiss Army Knife. I cut through the tape and opened the box. After I pulled out wads of packing, I found another, smaller box, enveloped in tape and surrounded with packing material. This one contained another smaller box also secured with tape. In the final box I found a parcel masked many times over in tape. In tape. In Technical Tape?

By this time, it had occurred to me that the package was from Technical Tape Incorporated. After carefully unwinding yards and yards of tape, I was finally able to unwrap the parcel. Inside I found a plaque, suitably framed for display, addressed as follows:

To Joryn Jenkins
The Prettiest & Youngest Stockholder of the Year
For Asking
The Best & Hardest Question

I realized years later that the certificate was signed at the bottom just like a college diploma, by the Chairman of the Board and the President of *Technical Tape Incorporated*.

To this day, the plaque hangs in a place of honor on my office wall. It's next to my Yale University Bachelor's Degree, my Georgetown Law Center Juris Doctorate, my photos with various of the justices of the Supreme Court of the United States, and the award that I received in 2001 in the Supreme Court itself, one of only two annually bestowed in that hallowed courtroom.

I'm certain that this plaque played a huge role in making me the person who I am today. I continue to be astonished by the amazing generosity that compelled these two gentlemen to recognize a small girl's courage and to reward it in the only way they could, with a tangible token of their acknowledgment and respect.

Chapter Three

Game Changer: Is the Collaborative Process Appropriate for You (Both)?

So I've been very convincing and you're already at the point where you're thinking that the collaborative process is really the only option that makes sense for you, whether you're headed for divorce, or simply establishing paternity for a child. Here are some questions that you should then ponder. And it might make sense to discuss the answers with the lawyer you propose to use.

1. Have you been divorced before?
   a. If so, does your spouse or partner know the details of that divorce?
   b. What exactly does she or he know?
   c. What process did you use then?
   d. How did that go?

2. Have you spoken with anyone who has been involved in the collaborative process?
   a. What did they tell you?
   b. Has your spouse?

3. Is there a history of a coercive or violent relationship with your spouse?
   a. Is there an extreme power imbalance between you?
   b. Is there a history of verbal abuse in your

relationship?
    c. Are you frightened of your spouse or partner?

4. Do either of you suffer from mental illness or a personality disorder?
    a. If so, would that person be willing to seek help?
    b. Have either of you been treated for anxiety, depression, ADD, or any other type of disorder?
    c. Have either of you taken medication for mental illness?
    d. Have either of you attended counseling?
    e. Do you believe that your spouse has an undiagnosed mental illness?
    f. Does your spouse believe that of you?

5. Are both of you able to empathize?
    a. When your spouse is sad or hurt, do you feel bad?
    b. Does the same hold true for your spouse?
    c. Are you and your spouse able to see issues from the other's perspective?
    d. Are you and your spouse each able to appreciate the contributions of the other to the marriage?

6. Do either of you suffer from any type of emotional problem?
    a. What type of problem?
    b. If so, would that person be willing to seek help?

7. Do either of you suffer from a substance abuse problem?
    a. If so, would that person be willing to seek help?
    b. Does one of you believe that the other party has a substance abuse problem?
    c. Does the other deny it?

8. Have either of you invaded the privacy of the other?
    a. Has either of you secretly spied on the other?
    b. Have you read your husband's e-mails without his permission?

    c. Have you hired a private investigator to follow your wife?

    d. Have you recorded your husband without his permission?

    e. Have you looked at your wife's phone records without her permission?

9. Is it possible for you or your spouse to cooperate in a team dynamic?

    a. Are you and your spouse able to trust the team?

    b. Have you or your spouse ever had a bad experience with another professional?

    c. During your marriage, how well were you and your spouse able to work with one another?

10. Are you able to trust your spouse?

    a. Can she or he trust you?

11. Are you willing to be transparent?

    a. Do you have a legitimate reason to doubt that your spouse will be transparent?

12. Are you or your spouse unwilling to share your interests and goals with one another?

    a. Are you willing to consider your spouse's interests and goals?

13. How receptive would your spouse be to your suggestions about the possibility of proceeding collaboratively?

    a. What about your suggestions as to how to find a collaborative lawyer?

    b. How open would she or he be to considering a list of lawyers with whom your choice of lawyer has had success in collaborative cases?

14. Do you or your spouse have unrealistic expectations as to what you will receive in divorce?

    a. Has one of you consulted with a trial lawyer about

what you might expect in your divorce?

b. Has that trial lawyer created unrealistic expectations in either you or your spouse?
c. What do you expect to receive?
d. What are your priorities in terms of what you would like most to accomplish?
e. What is most important to you?
f. What is your biggest concern regarding your divorce?
g. What would be the best case scenario for you?

15. Are you or your spouse seeking revenge?
   a. Do you or your spouse adamantly feel as though you need your day in court?
   b. If so, why?
   c. Do you hate one another?

If you answered these questions candidly, your replies should grease the wheels for a productive discussion with your choice of collaborative attorney as to whether the collaborative process option is a viable choice for you and your partner to consider.

Who the heck wants his personal information splashed all over the front page of the town newspaper? If you aren't committing a crime and you're not famous already, aren't you entitled to some privacy?

Well, I'd say "yes" under most circumstances, but not in my world. I'm a divorce lawyer and, if you choose to dissolve your marriage the traditional way, in a courtroom, then you've chosen to air your grievances in public, and the public has the right to "read all about it."

This is the story of one such divorce. When it was over, the husband, given that his personal information was now common knowledge in the town where he lived, moved back home to Belgium.

The Panties

A matronly, but petite Flemish woman with a heavy accent and a snaggletooth, and emanating the ripe scent of body odor, timidly entered our offices. Louise eventually retained our firm to represent her in her divorce. In addition, we assisted her in defending the petition for a domestic violence injunction that her husband had filed against her. This sweet, middle-aged woman had two concerns. One was her college-aged son, Liam, and the other, the children for whom she cared in her home-based daycare.

When her husband, Lars, a tall, brutish man, learned she planned to divorce him, he called the police, claiming she had punched him in the face. She explained, "Late one night, we were in bed. I was watching a program on my laptop, but he wanted me to turn it off so he could go to sleep. I said there were only five more minutes, and I wanted to finish it. Speck [her ten-pound Benjie dog] was cuddled next to me on the bed. Lars grabbed Speck by the neck and threw him out of the room! Then he yanked Splash (that's my lab) by the collar and shoved him out of the room, too."

I had my own dog in my lap as I listened to her tell her story, and I hugged her closer. "What happened next?"

"After he returned and tried to swat the laptop closed, I batted his hand away. When I did, my pinky and ring fingers brushed his left cheek. At that instant, he announced 'I love America' because he knew he could now have me arrested for battery. He threatened to call 911. He said it would be my last evening in the house."

"Had you injured him at all? Was he bleeding or bruised?"

"No, when he left the room, he wasn't bleeding or bruised. And there was no mark on my hand where he said I hit him."

"Was anyone else at home at the time? Did they hear the fight?"

"My parents and our son were in their bedrooms down the hallway, but they heard nothing. That's how harmless the fight was."

"But when the police arrived, his nose was bleeding a bit, and he had a loose front tooth. Lars has tooth implants, and they often come free."

"Did the officers believe that you had injured him?"

"No. The responding officer asked him if he really wanted to proceed with filing a police report." Given the disparity in their sizes, the officer must have wondered about the truthfulness of Lars' story. It would mean that Louise would go to jail, and that would affect her daycare business, which was their only income.

"What did Lars decide?"

"He initially decided not to proceed, but the officer explained that one of us *would* go to jail that night. If Lars didn't proceed against me, then the officer would have to take *him* to jail for making a false report. Not surprisingly, Lars chose for me go to jail for the night. At the battery hearing the next day, he dropped the matter, and I was released."

Unfortunately, this event caused much damage to the daycare business. Sweet Louise's mug shot was available to anyone who searched her name on-line. Who would continue to entrust their children to someone who had been arrested for battery? Although we got her record expunged, it was nearly impossible to have her mug shot permanently removed from the internet. Luckily, some clients liked her so much and had so much faith in her that they allowed their children to remain.

She immediately petitioned for divorce, despite her grave concerns about his possible response. Their marriage was a history of his verbal, emotional, and physical abuse.

When they lived in Belgium, he became angry with her because she refused to do something that he had asked, and he tried to kick her. When she jumped away, he accidentally kicked the cabinet door and broke his big toe.

After Liam's birth, Louise went to the hospital for a fairly routine surgery, and, unbeknownst to her, Lars instructed the doctor to sterilize her. Louise, who wanted a large family, didn't learn why she was never able to have more children until many years later.

He often kicked and hit her beloved dogs. He repeatedly released the dogs to wander in the neighborhood and then taunted her about it. He often victimized Liam, as well. Once when Louise and Liam ran after the dogs because Lars had let them out, Lars locked them both out of the house and then jeered at them through the sliding glass door. Liam finally used a code to enter the front of the house. When Lars realized that he was inside, he unlocked the sliding glass door for Louise, but then slammed her hard against the wall when she entered.

A couple of months later, when she was washing dishes, he threw a can at her, and it hit her in her back.

He said he'd rather kill her than see her with another man. After making this threat, he would remind her of the knife he kept in his nightstand. He also threatened to ruin her daycare business if she ever tried to divorce him.

Because of the history of violence and the incident that resulted in her arrest, Louise also petitioned for an injunction for protection against domestic violence from Lars. When she filed, she was told that, on the petition's face, there was insufficient evidence for a temporary injunction. However, the judge agreed to set a hearing in order to hear from both parties. It was an uphill battle to get the injunction. We persisted. She was very fearful of her husband's potential violence, including entering the marital home and upsetting her daycare children, doing something to harm her business, or picking a fight with Liam.

Although Lars had dropped the battery charges against her, she was convinced he wanted her out of the house so he could stay and ruin the daycare. He had begun by having her arrested. She was terrified of what else he would do if allowed to remain living there.

Often during divorce proceedings, one spouse will pretend there's domestic violence. This gives that spouse the upper hand in the divorce by establishing majority timesharing with minor children and/or getting the other spouse out of the house. When an injunction is entered, the "victim" is usually allowed to stay in the home and is granted temporary majority timesharing with the children. This affects the final judgment.

Normally, the living arrangements during the process of divorce become permanent. Therefore, winning an injunction early on strengthens the likelihood that that spouse will receive the marital home and the majority of timesharing. Usually it is the wife who employs this strategy, but sometimes, the husband tries to force the wife out of the home this way.

When prepping Louise for the hearing, we stressed the importance of convincing the judge that she was fearful for her own personal safety. During the hearing, we questioned her regarding the recent incident and the many past episodes of Lars' violence, aggression, and harassment. We also questioned Liam. It's not common to question a client's child on the stand, but Liam was over eighteen and passionate to protect his mother from his father.

To our relief, the judge granted her petition for protection, and an injunction was entered for one year. Because the proceedings continued beyond that year, the judge extended the injunction until the divorce was finalized.

Lars had rarely worked during the marriage, and most of their money came from Louise's work and her family. In Belgium, they had paid reduced taxes because she was considered a "helping wife"; she was married to Lars, who was "self-employed." If they had remained married, he would have received a larger government pension due to Louise's "helping wife" status. But, once divorced, he would only receive the normal pension. And she would receive no pension. She believed this additional money and support routinely received from her family were the reasons he wanted to remain married.

When they moved to the United States, Louise accidentally discovered he'd developed an interesting habit. Early one morning, when her daycare children were still eating breakfast, she quietly crept into her bedroom, trying not to wake him. She found him wearing her white bra. Although she was shocked, she postponed a discussion because the children and Liam were there in the kitchen.

When they did talk, she made it clear that she was very hurt by his behavior and would not accept it. She asked him to make a choice between the cross-dressing and their marriage. He assured her he wanted the marriage and he went to counseling a few times. Although he soon quit, he continued to promise her that he would abandon his cross-dressing activities.

But he didn't. She repeatedly found her panties with holes cut into them. Eventually she had to put a lock on her closet door so he couldn't steal her clothes. When she questioned him about finding women's undergarments in their home that weren't hers, as well as a wig with long hair and a pornographic magazine, he claimed he had found the items "on the street." Despite her objections, Lars frequently visited pornographic websites for men who dress as women.

Once the injunction was granted, he wasn't permitted to remain in their home. He had nowhere else to go, so he was forced to return to Belgium, where he still had family to support him. The case would have finished fairly quickly, except for the interference caused by the distance and the time difference. We finally scheduled his deposition to try to pressure him to settle.

Although his "habit" wasn't legally relevant to the dissolution, Louise very much wanted to ask him about it during the discussion. I waited until the end because I didn't want him to refuse to answer questions that *were* relevant. Because he was in Belgium, he appeared via Skype. He clearly had not informed his counsel about his peculiar "habit."

When I posed my first question to him on this matter, his attorney almost fell out of his chair in shock. Surprisingly, Lars responded with honesty and passion, clearly tortured by his cross-dressing desires. I've never worked so hard to maintain my professionalism as when I asked these embarrassingly personal questions. He responded with emotion and candor. Meanwhile, his attorney laughed hysterically and threw water bottle caps at me from across the room, outside the camera's view!

Ultimately, once Lars' attorney became aware of the details of their marriage, the divorce was mediated successfully. Louise retained her beloved daycare, and Lars relocated permanently to his country of origin. To this day, however, I wonder about how Liam resolved his own differences with his father.

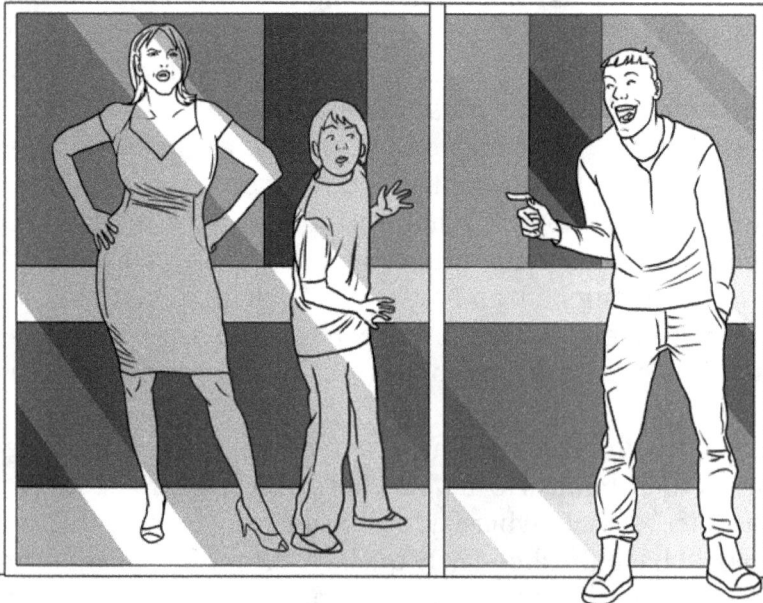

Then again, you might not have anything lewd or improper to hide from the public. But what if someone simply wanted to know your personal information so that he could target you somehow? That's what happened in my next story.

The Stalker

Mary was a tall, willowy brunette who had been married for 20 years to a very successful businessman here in Tampa. When he had his second affair with his second new secretary, she called it quits and asked him to move out, which he did, moving in with the secretary overnight.

I handled Mary's divorce and, ultimately, his attorney, a guy I'd worked "against" several times over the years, and I prevailed upon the couple to mediate their disputes before a judge was able to order them to do it. Although my client was very angry at her husband, given his infidelities, she understood that the law ignores such things, unless they impact on the marital finances or the children. Still, our discussion was not easy.

"I'm sure he spent our money on her." Mary frowned down at her hands; she wasn't happy that she had no recourse, but she was resigned.

"The accountant couldn't find any proof of that," I replied, matter-of-factly.

"He didn't take her on any trips... buy her any gifts at all?"

"Not that we could find." I considered. "And the fact of the matter is that the children were completely unaware of either of his affairs. So it's not like there was any bearing there."

"Thank God for that!" Mary was emphatic.

"Well, even if there had been, you wouldn't want to go to trial on that issue, unless it was really flagrant or destructive, like having sex right in front of the kids, or something along those lines." I explained, "It's not the sort of thing you want in the public record, so that your children can find out later what a jerk he was. In fact, you don't want the community knowing about it even now. It might affect his income... and therefore his ability to pay you alimony."

"Well, that's true."

So the four of us, Mary and her husband and both of us lawyers, met with the mediator, a gal who had been a highly respected, but aggressive trial lawyer until she burnt out on the whole litigation process and closed her law practice. It took the five of us ten hours to hash out an agreement, and another three on top of that to carefully structure the language of the written document.

I worried that, by the end of our marathon mediation session, the two clients would be too tired to comprehend what they were signing. John, especially, was giving Mary a handsome settlement, nothing she wasn't entitled to, but, by the same token, she wouldn't have to work for the rest of her life. Her child support alone would have taken care of a middle class family of four comfortably.

But a month later, John was still good with the agreement. They both accompanied me to the courthouse downtown where we obtained the judge's approval, and he executed the final judgment.

Eighteen months later, I ran into Mary, stylishly groomed, as always, at a nail salon where we were both having pedicures. When she noticed us waving at each other, her nail technician settled Mary in the chair next to mine, so that we could catch up.

Mary proceeded to tell me a chilling tale. About a year earlier, she had attended one of her children's soccer games at Jesuit High School here in town, and she ran into a man in the stands whose godson was also on the field. They struck up an amusing conversation and the guy had Mary in stitches the whole time.

When she ran into him again at the next soccer practice, the same thing happened again. It seemed they had an awful lot in common. When the game ended, he invited her for a cup of joe, and she willingly agreed.

The next morning, over their coffees at the local Starbucks, they chatted in the early April sunshine out at a sidewalk table. While folks hurried by on their way to work, Mary and Kenneth talked about soccer, about their mutual passion for the performing arts, about their addiction to reading (they both had their bachelor's degrees in English Literature!), about his regret that he had never been married and had not (yet) had children, and about her two wonderful boys, who were both now in high school.

Neither of them approved of recreational marijuana (nor had either of them tried it in college), but they both felt that medicinal marijuana should be approved by the legislature. Like her, he had been raised a Lutheran and still attended church, although not one to which she had ever been.

They had several acquaintances in common (although no close friends), and that they had never met before puzzled and intrigued her.

They arranged to meet again the next week. And then the week after that.

This man seemed like the perfect catch. He was charming, attractive, witty, and well-read, and her interest in him never paled with time. They had everything in common, and despite her efforts to find some point on which they might disagree, she never did. Several meet-ups later, when he asked her out to dinner, she was thrilled.

He took her to her favorite restaurant, although how he knew that it was her chosen eating establishment she had no idea. Their scintillating conversation continued, establishing even more points of commonality. When he took her home that night, he kissed her on the cheek. The perfect gentleman.

After several weeks of coffees and lunches when the boys were not around, she decided to introduce him to them, although not as anyone special, as "just a friend." She chose to do it at their next soccer match, and, interestingly, the boys and he had already met. In fact, he had helped to coach some of their games.

This guy was Prince Charming!

The boys took to him, and he to them. As she and he became closer, he would ask permission to take the boys out to lunch or to football games at Raymond James Stadium. The boys loved him, talking about him incessantly.

When he proposed, she didn't hesitate. "Yes," she whispered, happily.

She was in the midst of preparations for the wedding, albeit nothing very fancy, given that it was her second marriage. Her nuptials were just two weeks away when Jane, an acquaintance whom she'd invited, called to ask her out for a glass of wine and some "girl talk." Mary and Jane hadn't spoken for a while because Mary had been too absorbed in her romance with Kenneth, something she had not expected at the age of 42. But they were not close, so this was no surprise.

Nevertheless, Jane had called as soon as she'd received the invitation.

The conversation got off to a slow start. Jane seemed interested in getting caught up on current events and Mary was only too happy to describe her good fortune. After she described how she and Kenneth had met, how serendipitous it was that he had a godson at the same school as her sons and that he happened to be there whenever she was, how extraordinarily lucky she felt to have found a man with whom she had so much in common, Jane mentioned, examining her wine glass carefully, that she had known Kenneth for several years. Mary was perplexed. "You never introduced us?!"

"You were married. He was single. John and he had nothing in common, as far as I could tell. So why would I?" Jane paused. "We did talk about you at one point." She took a deep breath and held it for a moment.

Mary frowned. "Me? What do you mean?"

Jane released the breath she was holding with "Yes, you." She hesitated again and then spoke in a rush. "Ken and I both attended one of those South Tampa dinner parties last year. You know the kind I'm talking about. While we were there, Kenneth mentioned that he had been following your divorce very closely. I didn't tell him that I knew you, but he went on to say that he knew what kind of money John made because it was all right there in the court file for anyone to see, and that, when your divorce was final, if you got any kind of reasonable settlement, he had every intention of asking you out. Well, I *certainly* didn't mention that I knew you *then*!"

Jane observed the look of shock on Mary's face. "Hey, don't kill the messenger! I thought he'd just had a little too much to drink, especially when he confided that he'd always wanted to find a woman who was independently wealthy 'to support him in his old age.' But now I'm not so sure. Isn't all that information about your kids and their school and their soccer right there in the settlement agreement? Isn't the settlement agreement filed in the court file?"

It didn't take Mary long, replaying her conversations with Kenneth in her head, to realize that she was, in fact, being played. It was a terrible blow to her ego, but Mary had always been a strong woman, and she had a good support system, too.

Thank goodness Jane had warned her before it was too late to call off the wedding. Explaining to her sons was a bit harder, but the older one had already broken up with his first girlfriend, so he was understanding, and the younger one followed his lead.

Now she was sharing with me, so that I might understand the damage that publishing such private information in a court file can do and share it with you. Yet another reason not to litigate.

Chapter Four

25 Steps to Take Before Going to Court

The decision to hire a divorce attorney is a stressful one. Once you do, the process may quickly unfold before you have time to adequately prepare. Therefore, if you're going to court, before hiring an attorney, consider accomplishing the following:

1) Emotionally prepare yourself. Be certain that divorce is really what you want; it's difficult to turn back once those first steps have been taken, and certainly once the petition has been filed.

2) Consider counseling. Is your marriage salvageable? Have you tried everything? Would marriage counseling help? If not with a licensed mental health professional, perhaps with a friend. Perhaps with a religious counselor. Consider taking a class together to help your relationship.

Would your spouse be willing to try it? If so, try counseling before calling it quits. If offered the choice to do it again, many people would not file for divorce, so seriously consider ways that you might be able to save your marriage.

3) Ensure that you and your children are safe. If your spouse has ever been physically violent towards you or your children, or if she has a nasty streak, plan an escape route. If your spouse becomes violent towards you at any time, immediately call the police and file your injunction for protection against domestic violence as soon as you can.

Arrange for a safe retreat to which you and your children may retreat. If it's not safe to remain in your home, you may need to stay with friends or family, rent an apartment, or go to a shelter. Just be aware that if you leave the marital home, you may find it difficult to argue that you should be awarded the home in your divorce. Often courts will award the party who remains in the marital home the majority timesharing so that the children's lives are impacted as little as possible. Leave your home only if you are unsafe remaining there.

4) Open your own individual bank accounts in a new institution.

5) Arrange for a safe deposit box in the new institution. Give one key to a family member or a close personal friend. Hide your key.

6) Obtain a post office box. Arrange for any statements and correspondence from the new bank to be sent to the PO box or a new e-mail address.

7) Take half of the funds out of your joint accounts. In Florida, as in many venues, divorcing spouses share marital funds equally, regardless of who earned them or in whose name they are listed. Thus they each own 100% of the marital portion of the assets.

The marital portion is generally the amount acquired from the date of the marriage until the date when the divorce petition is filed. So how do you fairly share 100% of what you both own together? You remove half of those funds, and leave the other half for your spouse. Place the funds you've removed into your new individual account.

8) Open new credit cards in your name alone and arrange for bills and correspondence to go to the PO box or your new e-mail address.

9) Remove half of any bullion or collections you both own and place it in your safe deposit box.

10) Sever credit ties. Separate your shared credit card accounts. If your spouse is an authorized user on one of your cards, ask the issuer to remove your spouse's name. If you're joint users, freezing the cards may be your best bet. But wait to do this until right before making the big announcement. Otherwise, the jig's up as soon as your spouse swipes.

11) Open new bank accounts in new banking institutions.

Place the money you take from your joint accounts into your new account so that your spouse can't access those funds. Arrange for your paycheck to be deposited in that account rather than your old joint account. Once you file for divorce, you should be able to keep all of the money that you earn as long as you don't use marital funds to earn it, unless you're paying alimony, of course.

12) Take your personal computer to an expert and have it cleaned of all information that you don't want your spouse to see.

13) Change all of your passwords and, if necessary, keep records of your new passwords in your safe deposit box.

14) Make any changes necessary to your designations of life insurance beneficiaries and powers of attorney. Change the "payable on death" beneficiary on your accounts so that your spouse will not automatically receive your funds if you pass away during the divorce process.

15) Copy important documents, bank records, retirement accounts, deeds, insurance policies, etc. Be a snoop. As financial statements come each month, begin to make copies of those documents, not only so that you have the documents that you need for your mandatory discovery, but also so that you are aware of places where your spouse may be hiding money. If you're able to do so safely, look through his or her computer, phone, filing cabinets, etc., and make copies of anything that you feel may be relevant to your divorce.

Place those copies in your safe deposit box. Begin gathering copies of any documents that verify assets, liabilities, income and expenses, including recent bank, brokerage and retirement statements, tax returns, and real estate deeds — and the prenuptial agreement, if you have one. This step can take three to six months, depending on how accessible the documents are. Having a paper trail saves stress, time, and money. You won't be captive to your spouse, hoping that he or she will provide copies to you, nor will you have to pay your lawyer to find this information.

16) Place your personal valuable jewelry in your safe deposit box, as well as any gifts made to you individually by other people.

17) Make a list of your personal property, especially if you are planning on leaving the marital home. List everything in your home. List your jewelry, your clothes, your art, your kitchen items,

your art, your furniture, your DVDs, your books, your CDs, your electronics . . . everything. Make a separate list of what you think belongs to your spouse. If you do leave, it will be hard to remember everything that you have, and you are entitled to half of the marital personal property. And people rarely realize what belongs to them jointly with their spouse and what is separate.

18) Video record the contents of your house, especially collections of stamps, coins, art, antiques, etc. Place the videos in your safe deposit box.

19) Consider what timesharing schedule would be appropriate for your family. Perhaps talk to a counselor who specializes in the developmental stages of children to get an opinion on what would be best for them.

20) Close your social media websites like Facebook and Twitter. Divorcing spouses often use information found on these websites against one another in court.

21) Hide your crazy! Remember that you are about to be under a microscope, so while you may feel like you are losing control, it is important to remain level-headed. You don't want to give your spouse anything to use against you in court. And your children need a sane parent. (Preferably two.)

22) Get help for your children if they are having a hard time coping with your divorce.

23) Stash some cash. Ideally, you should have a year's worth of basic living expenses in a personal account prior to filing. If all of your money is co-mingled and you have no way of opening your own account without raising red flags, open a credit card with a low or introductory 0% interest rate.

This step is important because divorce proceedings often take six months or more, during which time you may lose access to spousal support. Plus, you'll need to lay out another $10,000 to $20,000 for an initial retainer if you plan to work with an attorney and/or a financial advisor. (If you earn significantly less than your spouse or have no income, you'll still need a retainer to fund a lawyer to petition to have your spouse pay ongoing legal fees.)

24) Arrange for payment of attorney's fees and court costs. Divorces are expensive. If you don't have liquid assets available, ask family or friends for loans. Or open a low interest credit card

before the authorities become aware of the compromise to your credit caused by divorce.

25) Finally, and most importantly, now that you understand the horrendous list of pre-court tasks, consider courtless divorce options like collaborative divorce or mediation. Interview attorneys who specialize in these alternatives, as well as litigation attorneys, so that you choose the option that is best for you and your family. And, when the time comes, discuss the choice of process with your spouse; if you both choose collaborative divorce, you have the best chance of restructuring your family successfully. If you cannot agree on the process, then you will be stuck with the default . . . courtroom divorce, which is more expensive, more time-consuming, and more destructive than any other choice of process.

Chapter Five

Interview a Collaborative Practitioner

So you've decided you want to move forward with collaboratively dissolving your marriage. What now?

Well, before you retain a collaborative divorce lawyer, before you identify the collaborative financial neutral and/or facilitator for inclusion on your team, before you decide on other neutral professionals who you might want for your team, consider posing these questions of the candidates. If you do, listen closely to the answers. This interview should aid in your quest for the right team members.

Suggest that your soon-to-be-ex spouse do the same.

1. How do people getting divorced from each other "collaborate?" How can people who are truly in conflict "negotiate" without using intimidation, threats, and ultimatums to get what they want?

Collaborative practice is *not* about the two spouses "cooperating," which is a preconceived idea with which some have approached me. It *is* about the two participants working together on a team which includes neutral professionals, as well as their own specially-trained attorneys, joining forces to problem solve the issues raised and to brainstorm the options possible in the dissolution of their marriage. Yes, of course, they can "collaborate."

Most important to the collaborative process, and the critical reason why most collaborative divorces are successful, is the approach the team takes to the issues. Positions are *not* the issues; interests *are*. A professional who understands collaborative practice will explain the difference between a position and an interest to you.

Taking a position is the same as insisting on a specific outcome. That's the "line in the sand." Negotiating *interests* is about being open to different outcomes that can meet that underlying interest. Interest-based negotiations help divorcing spouses to identify their goals, as opposed to the single option that would traditionally be set forth in a settlement offer. By encouraging each spouse to define his or her goals, the team can begin to generate multiple settlement options that could accomplish the goal. This helps divorcing spouses see that there isn't just one way to settle, and it gives everyone more bargaining room. It helps clients see the forest, not just the trees. It sometimes can be used to "enlarge the pie," as well, creating options that might not be available in the traditional divorce paradigm.

Collaborative lawyers encourage their clients to discover, identify, and then articulate their interests, rather than to take positions. Although taking a position is the more natural reaction in any conflict, i.e. to identify the most obvious beneficial outcome and to latch onto it, it can be a "red herring," that, were the client to achieve it, might leave the client unhappy when all is said and done.

The neutral professionals on the collaborative team also work with the clients to identify their goals, asking the clients to define their goals early in the process. This process opens up options and often clears a path to an outcome that can meet both participants' individual goals.

2. How do you deal with roadblocks in the negotiations? What if my spouse refuses to budge on a certain issue, effectively delivering an ultimatum to *me*?

The collaborative professional should explain that the team will work together with the clients to uncover each spouse's underlying interest behind a position she or he has taken, and will try to reach a resolution that satisfies that interest. Positional bargaining versus interest-based bargaining is a fundamental shift in thinking which lets go of labels in favor of the bigger picture. It seeks to enlarge the range of alternatives so that the needs of all participants are addressed and met to the greatest extent possible. *The key to resolution is to link the solution to the underlying issue to be solved.*

3. How does one choose a collaborative attorney? Ask yourself if the attorney you're interviewing is a "pit bull?"

If the answer is "yes," he isn't a collaborative attorney! If the approach is to turn everything into a fight or be opportunistically adversarial, he can't be a collaborative attorney. There's a great deal more to being an effective advocate than simply being aggressive and a collaborative attorney understands that. When you retain a pit bull, you pay for all the fighting he's doing in your case, and pit bulls usually fight about anything and everything, which gets very expensive very quickly. Collaborative practice seeks to avoid unnecessary waste of time and of money, and eliminate the concomitant stress.

If your initial consultation reveals a strategy based on manipulation, maneuvering, threat of court, sandbagging, or any other such malicious acts, then you should question whether this attorney employs a spirit of collaboration. Someone suggesting these strategies isn't committed to the collaborative process. Such acts will likely anger your spouse, and potentially cause the process to break down in the future, forcing a reset, and a resulting loss of both time and money.

4. Ask these questions. What's your collaborative experience? Are you a member of any collaborative practice groups? What types of trainings have you had? How many participation agreements have you signed?

It shouldn't take much time for on-line research on the associations of collaborative professionals in your area. If there aren't any, at the very least, your professional should be a member of IACP, the International Academy of Collaborative Professionals. Membership in these types of groups can help you determine if someone is committed to working in the collaborative process and engaged in ongoing training.

That being said, the lack of training or participation doesn't mean that he wouldn't make an excellent and effective collaborative professional. If yours, for example, is already highly involved in other forms of alternative dispute resolution, such as mediation, he may not yet have had the opportunity to become collaboratively trained. If he is open to the idea of collaboration but not yet trained or a member of a group, ask if he'd like to talk with your attorney, or, if you are interviewing an attorney, your spouse's attorney about the process. If your spouse has already enlisted the aid of a collaboratively-trained attorney, that lawyer will likely welcome the chance to open another lawyer's eyes to this process.

5. What other professionals will be part of our collaborative divorce team? How is that decided and who decides how the duties are assigned?

If you are interviewing counsel, you should be certain that your collaborative attorney understands the benefits of working with neutral collaborative professionals, so that the both participants receive the benefit of all of the professionals' strengths. Ask your attorney about both positive and negative experiences she has had working with the different collaborative team members who may be involved in your collaborative divorce. Be specific. Ask follow-up questions so that you can truly gauge the attorney's commitment to the process. These team professionals usually include:

> Financial neutrals or facilitators (in some venues, the facilitators are the financial neutrals) who work to clarify each party's financial interests and help to structure an agreement that meets each party's financial goals; experts at completing budgets, profit & loss analyses, financial statements, and . . .

Mental health facilitators or coaches (in some venues, both spouses have their own coaches) who concentrate on eliminating the stressful communication and emotional issues that can commandeer the negotiation process; and . . .

Attorneys who, while "representing" the other party, will participate on the divorce team to negotiate an agreement that meets both parties' interests; and sometimes . . .

Child specialists who work to bring the voice of the child into the negotiations.

The team may also include:

Mediators, neutral participants who specialize in negotiations between the divorcing spouses;

Vocational experts, neutral participants who analyze a party's career options and earning capacity;

Neutral corporate, tax, and estate planning attorneys who may assist in answering questions about specific issues in your case and who may suggest creative alternatives that the rest of the team may not be trained to recognize and propose;

Neutral business, real estate, and personal property appraisers who can help you determine the value of property in the marital estate;

Insurance consultants, neutral professionals who can advise you on your insurance options;

Certified financial planners, either neutral or working for just one party, who can recommend options for handling finances after the divorce;

Estate planners who can prepare post-divorce will and trust documents;

Mortgage brokers who can advise you as to your options regarding any mortgages you both or each may have;

Realtors who can list your marital and extra-marital real property for sale; and

Divorce coaches who may not be neutral, but can help guide one or both of you through the very emotional divorce process.

Truly collaborative professionals can give you examples of how their previous clients have reaped the benefits of employing these specialized professionals on their teams, and how their divorces generally proceeded more smoothly as a result. Better still, listen for amazing stories about the unexpected rewards or the astonishing epiphanies that their clients may have realized in or enjoyed because of the process.

I tell some of the stories about those remarkable moments in this book, many of which occurred in my own practice. In fact, it is safe to say that, in three out of four of my collaborative divorces, there came a time when something happened that made my skin prickle, the hair on my arms stand up, and my heart swell to ten times its normal size, and it was everything I could do to prevent the tears from spilling.

Working as a professional on a collaborative divorce team is a gratifying experience. It is always more beneficial to work with colleagues toward common goals without the pressure of trying to gain the upper hand (which is what litigation is all about). Many collaborative professionals have worked together before (given how small the community is) and that is even better for the participants because the professionals enjoy a camaraderie that will assuredly grease the wheels of peaceful negotiations.

6. If you're still interviewing lawyers, pose this question. My husband gave me a large packet of information his attorney gave him about collaborative divorce, and I found your name in the listing of attorneys in the same "Collaborative Group." You obviously know one another well. Won't you concede to demands my spouse's attorney makes for fear of damaging your relationship with him?

The answer should be "No. As your attorney, I represent your interests." Collaborative attorneys understand that the attorneys must do so for their clients. It is a benefit to the participants for attorneys who work well with one another and trust one another to be on their collaborative team.

7. Do you care whether my spouse gets what he or she wants out of this divorce?

Does the professional truly understand the difference between collaboration and cooperation? Collaboration is about ensuring that the other person's interests are met, even if they aren't the same as yours. This is arguably more difficult than working together for mutual benefit toward common goals, which is what cooperation is all about.

Collaboration is about meeting the needs and serving the best interests of everyone involved. It is likely that each party will not get everything she wants. If you are interviewing the lawyer, your attorney's job is to protect your interests in a fair way while also working with the team to satisfy your spouse's interests. The result is that, on occasion, you may feel that your attorney is being overly caring of your spouse's concerns.

There aren't many couples who share common goals at the end of their marriage. The lack of common objectives is, after all, what has led them to divorce. While they may be equally committed to protecting their kids from the fireworks of their conflict and to outwardly maintaining an amicable relationship with each other for that reason, they rarely have common financial goals for their lives after divorce.

After all, financial issues are the most common reason that folks dissolve their marriages. One may feel that owning his own home is critical, while the other is quite happy letting her landlord worry about maintenance issues. One may feel that his business is taking off and will fly, if he can just commit some serious time to it, while the other knows that she's about to hit her head on a glass ceiling. One may want to enjoy spending her earnings, while the other needs to put that money towards his retirement.

Agreeing to work collaboratively at the beginning of the process requires each party to both respect the other's concerns and interests, and also understand that an agreement cannot be signed until each of their goals are met.

And, by the way, ultimately, your collaborative attorney, like you, should understand that your future relationships with your spouse and your children are important considerations, not just the financial ones.

8. Don't spouses become more bound up in the process for fear of it failing and having to start over? How do I ensure that the attorneys are not taking advantage of this once we are deeply invested? What can I do if I feel my spouse's collaborative attorney is taking advantage of the system?

The participants' pledge not to litigate is a crucial component of the collaborative process. Because of this pledge, the spouses are able to speak freely without worrying that what she or he says may be used against him or her in court. This approach creates a "safe" environment in which the team can help both of the spouses to negotiate. Because the commitment not to go to court is a formal written agreement rather than just a verbal promise, it builds more trust in the collaborative process, which helps both of the participants get the results they want. The pledge encourages people to work towards a settlement instead of giving up on the process, relinquishing their attorneys, and litigating. But that's a positive because in the vast majority of cases, reaching a settlement is a better alternative than going to court.

The collaborative process eliminates the lawyer's ability to "stir the pot," whether by design or accidentally. The lawyer's sole job in the collaborative model is to help the clients satisfy their interests and settle the issues raised by the dissolution of their marriage. If he fails in that task and the collaboration terminates, then he is off the case. If he is "churning the case," you should immediately discuss your concern with your neutral facilitator so that she can address the problem with the team members.

9. My spouse is mentally ill. Can the collaborative process work for us?

Most of the time, the answer should be "yes." I recently heard a statistic (on national television) that one out of six Americans suffers from some form of mental illness. When one considers that depression and addiction are forms of mental illness, one begins to realize that this statistic is not unrealistic.

Divorce is one of the most stressful events that will occur in a person's life. And it is usually coupled with additional stresses, moving out of one's home being the most obvious. Of course, the divorce process itself can trigger mental illness in the person involved.

How then does one divorce someone who is mentally ill? Some laws that require that your spouse be competent before you can divorce him, or at least impose a waiting period before you can do so. One also must be competent to sign an agreement before it can be enforceable. Attorneys with a collaborative mindset will explain to you that, when a party is mentally ill, collaborative practice is likely the best alternative because a mental health professional participates in the process as either a coach or a facilitator. That person can help the team understand how best to work with the mentally ill client.

That said, the mental health professional will also better understand if a party is too ill to proceed.

10.   Is there a standard amount of time that is takes to complete a divorce collaboratively? Does a collaborative divorce take less time than a litigated courtroom divorce?

There is no set amount of time. Each situation is different.

However, with collaborative divorce there are no delays due to the court calendar being booked up, there are none of the typical back-and-forth time-consuming battles of lawyers speaking on behalf of the spouses, there are none of the drawn-out and/or extended deadlines for discovery and responses, etc. Comparatively, collaborative divorces are completed more quickly, in about a third of the time as courtroom divorces.

11.   What does a collaborative divorce cost? Is it less than a litigated divorce?

While statistics haven't been collected and collated to support this, in my experience a collaborative divorce costs less, overall, than a litigated divorce. One can easily see why this would be so, in the collaborative setting:

> There is one neutral expert for every issue, instead of a battle of two experts, and the expert needs only to prepare his opinion and recommendations, instead of also preparing to defend that opinion;

> Neutral, less expensive specialists perform tasks that highly paid attorneys would otherwise undertake, such as computing child support and completing the clients' financial affidavits;

> Neutral specialists meet with the clients on their own; in litigation, the attorneys would attend every meeting with their expert, and they would bill those joint meetings at their normal hourly rates;

> Discovery is a matter of a simple request, made in person, or perhaps by telephone or e-mail, instead of via expensive piles of lengthy court pleadings such as "requests for production," "interrogatories," and "subpoenas *duces tecum*"; and

> Discovery is also transparent, so no expensive

guessing games, no "hiding the pea under the shell," and no costly motions to compel discovery and for contempt for failure to comply.

These are the most readily apparent savings opportunities. The average collaborative case in my experience has run about $32,000 (total, for all of the professionals on the team) for the family, whereas a traditional courtroom divorce can cost you $100,000 just to get to the courthouse steps. And that's for *each* of you, husband and wife. (These figures will, of course, vary by jurisdiction and community.) Add to that the cost of the trial and you've spent a small fortune. And the only thing you've learned is how to go to battle.

12. What happens if, after the divorce is final, there are issues or disagreements that arise between my former spouse and me? Can those be handled collaboratively, as well?

Yes, if there is a post-judgment issue, the spouses may hire the team again to help resolve that issue. Often, participants include a provision in their marital settlement agreement that, if there is a post-judgment issue, the participants will attempt to resolve it collaboratively, rather than instantly seeking court intervention.

13. How does collaborative divorce relate to "conscious uncoupling?"

Conscious uncoupling is a method that spouses use to deal with the divorce, both emotionally and mentally. There is no legal component. Collaborative divorce helps participants maneuver through the legal and financial aspects of their divorce while still nurturing their emotional and mental well-being.

14. If my spouse and I have agreed on certain things beforehand, will they be deemed "settled," or can they still be used as negotiating points? How do we address issues that we agree upon during the collaborative process, but before everything is considered "settled"? How can I ensure decided issues aren't

continued to be used as negotiating points?

If you have settled some issues, ask the attorneys to draft those into agreements now rather than holding them back for negotiating chips. If it is a true collaboration, then drafting settled terms as they are agreed upon is reasonable.

In sum, knowing that your professional is committed to the collaborative mindset is essential to the success of the process. These questions will enable you to weed out the committed collaborative professionals from the dabblers and help you to trust that the process will move forward in the manner you envision.

Indeed, collaborative professionals working together often form their own closely-knit communities. And, when working together with the divorcing spouses, it has been our experience that the team truly creates "a village that can problem-solve a divorce." The dynamic that the collaborative team generates, both the professionals and the spouses, is not only unique, but is also a force with which to be reckoned.

Serendipity

Like-minded people hang out together. I attended a seminar in Miami for collaborative professionals with my associate. Having travelled from Tampa, we were the only out-of-towners at the seminar with just 36 other attendees. About halfway through the morning session, I noticed the name tag in front of the guy two seats over; he was the psychologist I had hired 15 years earlier as an expert in my husband's post-divorce nightmare litigation against his ex-wife.

Todd's divorce had taken place in Miami. But how many divorce lawyers, psychologists, and accountants were there in the area? And how serendipitous that one of the 36 in the room with me was this guy!

But wait . . . there's more! During the break, one of the accountants in the audience approached me, with his right hand held out. As we shook, he said, "My brother-in-law is a CPA in Tampa. I wonder if you know him."

"What's his name?"

"Bob Kokol."

I smiled, surprised. "How very odd. Bob and I just started a collaborative divorce case together, this week. Our first together!" How serendipitous, I thought.

But that still wasn't the end of the story. Right on this guy's heels was an attractive brunette, who stood behind him, waiting to chat with me. (Yes, I *did* feel like a celebrity!)

After introductions, she asked, "My brother practices law in Tampa. I thought you might know him, Richard Wilkes?"

Now I *was* surprised. "Sure do. Richard and I dated 25 years ago."

Attorneys can be the most difficult clients because they know too much for their own good. And a litigator, even as the client, may have a hard time stepping out of that trial attorney role, especially when he hasn't been trained in the collaborative process. So, although lawyers seek out my collaborative services more often than any other profession (because they *know* they don't want to air their issues in court), it can be more challenging to have a trial attorney as a collaborative client. However, once he realizes the benefits of the process, it becomes an eye-opening experience.

The Litigator

An old friend of mine, Byron Carter, a tall, jovial man, sought my representation just a few days after he had moved out of the home he shared with Dani, his wife of thirty years. Despite his imposing size, he had such a gentle, sincere smile that he didn't come across as menacing. Quick to point out his graying hair, he was proud to point out that at least he still had a full head of hair. Although by profession a trial attorney, he admitted that, in his personal life, he was a "conflict avoider." Wishing to avoid a confrontation with Dani, he left one night while she was out with her girlfriends.

While I gave Byron a tour of my office, he announced that he understood that I was one of the few attorneys in town who offered collaborative services. "I want a collaborative divorce," he declared.

Dani, a tall, handsome woman, had been shocked when he walked out. Although they'd had their problems throughout their entire marriage, as a traditional and religious woman, she had expected to remain married for life. Without any warning or discussion, Byron had walked out of her life with his clothes, some gold coins, a few guitars, and $250,000 from the $500,000 in their savings account. Despite the fact that she was an intelligent, educated woman who'd worked as a bonds trader when they first met, she'd been a stay-at-home wife for the last 25 years. And although their only child was in college, she still defined herself in that role.

Byron had engaged in numerous affairs throughout their' marriage. Eventually, he was diagnosed with and received treatment for a sexual addiction. His affairs had pushed Dani away, making her less physically affectionate. The more that retreated from his sexual advances, the more he sought sex with other women. It was a vicious cycle. Seeking revenge for the pain that Byron's affairs caused her, Dani had her own affair during the marriage.

Byron believed that they'd never shared an intimate connection, causing him to constantly seek one elsewhere. She thought that the only reason he had left because he was romantically involved with another woman.

A couple of years earlier, during the real estate bust, he'd been devastated when it became public knowledge that he and his law partner had defaulted on a sand mine investment. Though he was forced to file for bankruptcy, he was able to protect most of their assets because they were all marital. Dani felt especially betrayed because he left the day after the bankruptcy was discharged. It seemed he'd only stayed for financial reasons and had then discarded her.

Feeling wronged, she was highly emotional, vacillating between crying easily and becoming irate, in shock and grieving the demise of her marriage. She still felt rejection because of his unexplained serial adultery. Her Christian patience and forgiveness hadn't been enough; he'd still abandoned her.

He felt guilty but was convinced that he should be free to live and to love as he wished. While he wanted to be fair, even generous, he was desperate to move on as quickly as possible. He wanted to avoid Dani and her questions, yet maintain a good ongoing relationship with her, for the sake of their son.

Prior to the first full team meeting, the facilitator, Alicia, warned us to stick to the collaborative process as defined by the Carters' goals and to be clear about what was relevant. She assured us that the team structure would help them get through their issues without going down explosive rabbit trails. "Avoid the word 'fair,'" she admonished, wagging her finger at us. "It will absolutely set Dani off."

We met at the office of the financial professional, Christine, professionally decorated environment with rich leather chairs and artwork from local artists, it exuded a welcoming, homey feel. The walls were painted in warm, calming colors. The conference room was large enough for the team, but not so large as to be intimidating. The offices smelled citrusy, and there were bowls of chocolates in each one, as well as in the conference room where we gathered. She immediately offered us drinks and made us feel comfortable.

After our pre-brief, and before the full team meeting, each attorney met with her client privately to address any pre-meeting concerns and to answer any questions. "Forewarned is forearmed." Byron and I discussed the fact that Dani might be very emotional because she hadn't expected the divorce, and was still in the throes of grieving. I advised him against jumping to conclusions, which had done during our initial preparations.

His blunder hadn't been public to the team, much less to his wife, thank goodness. There had been an early, but urgent issue about liquidating one of the Carters' life insurance policies before its value was used to fund the annual $30,000 premium, sometime in the next couple of weeks, before our full team was to meet. Byron believed that it was the best financial decision for the couple to make, but Dani was fighting it simply because she was uneducated as to *why* it was a good decision. Therefore, prior to our first meeting, she had met with Christine to discuss it and to try to resolve it.

Despite the fact that Byron wanted to liquidate the insurance, he was upset when Dani had unilaterally emailed the insurance agent asking *how* it would be done. He sent me an angry email. "Is this the way this will go? I don't act but rather get everyone to weigh in and she just decides how things will come down and directs the agent to take action on a policy in my name and under my control? I think the next time I will just do what I want and backfill the team after."

I calmly suggested he suspend judgment. Dani had probably met with Christine, the financial neutral, who had explained to her why it made sense to liquidate the policy. Once she understood, it was likely she had simply acquiesced without telling him directly. Because everyone was under the (correct) impression that he wanted to cash in the policy, she probably just wanted to ensure that we had everything we needed to do so at the first team meeting. "It doesn't sound like she really did anything except give the guy a heads up. Am I missing something here? I saw this as a 'win.'"

Byron response made me aware that he, too, was still sensitive to Dani's decisions and opinions, and her tendency to try to control him. I warned him, "Don't assume that anything is going on without you knowing about it. If there's anything you want to know that's relevant, just ask, and you'll be told. If either of you has emotions to vent, don't assume that we're agreeing because we nod. We're simply acknowledging her feelings, not affirming her opinions. Don't read each nod as agreement."

Then we headed into the conference room. I approached Dani, whom I had known years ago, and reached out to shake her hand. She was a striking woman, perhaps 6 feet tall, a bit on the matronly side, and probably 30 pounds more than she used to weigh when she was 30. She smiled and remarked on how young I still looked. She didn't look much older than she did 30 years ago when we were acquaintances. Her hair was the same length as mine, just past the shoulders, and she must have as good a hairdresser as I do; it was a dark shade of blonde without a gray hair in it.

Because it was the first meeting, we reviewed the participation agreement with the Carters and had them sign it. While some attorneys want the team to read the entire agreement to the parties, asking as they go whether they understand and agree to each provision, it's tedious, and the parties tend to "zone out" and not really listen. In addition, they may become stressed because they're paying all of the professionals for this mind-numbing review. So many professionals forego the full reading and summarize each section in a more conversational format, checking often to be sure the parties understand and agree. Because our clients were both extremely well educated and had already reviewed the agreement with their attorneys, we chose to explain the salient points of the agreement, rather than suffer through the full reading.

Based on Alicia's advice that it was crucial for the Carters to stick to the agenda, we scripted every step of the entire meeting to avoid unanticipated surprises. One reason the Carters were getting divorced was because Dani was a control freak, and Byron was sick of her micromanaging his every move. Therefore, maintaining control for the sake of these two clients was imperative.

Once the Carters signed the participation agreement, we moved onto the first issue, determining how the professionals would be paid. When Byron moved out, he had divided the $500,000 in the savings account in two, leaving Dani with $250,000. He'd also left her an additional $30,000 in the checking account. By the way, she also had an additional $300,000 in a separate checking account that she inherited from her parents. This was all the liquid cash; they had other assets in various 401(k)s and IRAs and stocks, as well as gold coins and collectible guitars that Byron had also divided in half when he moved out.

Since his departure, he'd ignored her inquiries into how much he was making and where he was putting that money, which he had been depositing into a separate checking account he started the day after he left.

The question of paying the professional fees raised the issue that Dani was unwilling to delve into the $250,000 Byron left with her to pay ongoing expenses. The way he saw it, she was hoarding that money. In the meantime, he had already expended $40,000 of his $250,000 just to pay the legal fees for his attorney, me, and the bankruptcy attorney who had just put the finishing touches to his personal bankruptcy.

Meanwhile, she was bouncing checks because she refused to spend any of her $250,000. It frustrated Byron that she expected him to pay her ongoing expenses, despite that she was receiving all of the income from their rental properties.

The facilitator, Alicia, quickly perceived that the Carters were becoming upset over paying the professionals. Because each of them had already paid their attorney a retainer, Byron suggested that they each pay half of each professional's retainer. When Dani started crying, the facilitator called a break.

He and I remained in the conference room; everyone else left. I proposed that Christine remain with us to discuss alternatives to those already suggested, but Byron asked her to leave; he was especially sensitive to the fact that the neutrals might be able to share his comments to them with his wife and with Eileen, her lawyer.

I suggested that he front all the money, because we all could rely on the fact that the financial neutral would wrangle the numbers and, in the end, Byron would receive credit for having paid marital expenses out of his half of the marital funds. He resented being asked to do that, and I could see why. I was at a loss as to how to recommend going forward.

Then the light dawned.

"Byron, you're planning on this going to trial, aren't you?" I watched his face for acknowledgement. "You don't want to rely on a judge giving you credit for having fronted all this money because you know we can't rely on a judge to do anything 'fair.' Am I right?"

He leaned back in his chair and threw his arms wide, figuratively throwing himself on my mercy. "Well, no, I'm just worried that if we do hit an impasse, I won't get credit for all of this money that I'm putting out. And let's not forget I already spent $40,000 on marital expenses out of my share of the savings account."

I smiled. Why hadn't I anticipated that? Of course, he would "hope for the best but plan for the worst" possible outcome. That's what we trial lawyers do. And while the collaborative process is intended to eliminate the need to do that, he wouldn't know that being unschooled in the collaborative art.

I chided him. "Byron, you have to commit yourself to this

process. We all signed the agreement so that we wouldn't have to plan for trial." As I sighed, it occurred to me. "What if we entered into a partial agreement regarding the payments only, that they will be accounted for in the final divvying up of assets and liabilities? Any partial agreements that are signed *must* be approved by the judge as part of the final judgment."

By now, he was too stressed to consider this option, but when I suggested that we invite Christine into the discussion, he acquiesced. My associate, Lori, rounded her up.

I explained the problem to Christine and the options that we had considered.

She said, "Byron, perhaps I'm being too simplistic, but you were planning on liquidating that life insurance policy anyway. I talked to Dani about it, and she agreed. In fact, I suggested that she contact the administrator to satisfy herself on how the two of you would liquidate that insurance, and I believe she's already done that."

(That made me smile. Correct again.)

"Why don't we use that money to pay the professionals, as well as to pay your son's $35,000 college tuition for next year, which is also an item that Dani had denominated as an emergency? We can put the balance in a separate account to be used for expenses like this during the collaborative process."

Byron sat up, attentive.

I smiled, addressing Christine again. "Doesn't it make sense to take $40,000 of that life insurance proceeds and pay that back into Byron's half of the savings since he already spent that on marital expenses and Dani spent none of her share of the savings? Then he'd be whole, and they'd each have the $250,000 nest egg still protected."

He nodded. "I could do that."

Ultimately, we agreed that this made sense. He wanted Christine to float the idea, but she and I agreed that, because it was such a good idea, he should proffer it and get the credit for it. (Later, Dani's attorney clued us in later that she took this the wrong way, perceiving that it wasn't a magnanimous gesture, but a ploy to show himself off as "Lord of the Manor." However, Alicia praised the team for encouraging him to make the offer.) When

Byron did, she pondered it a moment, but was clearly headed in the wrong direction.

Byron immediately followed up with, "Why don't we split the balance of what remains? I can have $35,000, and she can have $35,000, instead of replacing my entire $40,000, and she only gets $30,000."

They finally agreed on that solution, resolving all of the substantive issues that had been scheduled for that meeting. I realized later that my trial attorney client had still been preparing for court, "just in case." They evenly split the life insurance, paying the specified joint expenses, and splitting the balance, but he is *still* owed reimbursement for the $40,000 he paid early on for mutual expenses.

Chapter Six

The Facilitator

Whether the financial neutral in the "two-coach model" or the mental health professional (often referenced as the "MHP") in the "one coach model," the facilitator plays an important role, if not the most important one in the collaborative process. She brings a specific skill set that assists the team to establish an atmosphere of cooperation, respect, and reasonableness. The facilitator runs the meetings, watches the time, keeps the team on track, and helps to maximize the process and outcomes.

If the facilitator is an MHP, during the process, she assists the clients in learning negotiation skills, often monitors the clients' emotional well-being, and will likely teach them better problem solving and more effective communication strategies. She may employ various approaches to enhance the collaborative team members' effectiveness. If children are involved, she'll likely assist them in recognizing and coordinating their respective parenting styles to enhance their future co-parenting relationship. If a child specialist isn't a team member, the facilitator will help them with their parenting plan.

With or without children involved, the MHP facilitator plays a crucial role because she assists them in achieving acceptable outcomes, taking into consideration their expressed goals, interests, and concerns. Because she's trained in human behavior, communication skills, personalities, etc., she's more able than the other professionals to defuse destructive situations and prevent progress-halting situations from developing and commandeering the process.

Depending on whether the team opts for a one-coach or two-coach model, the MHP may or may not act as the neutral facilitator. Generally, communities have their own protocols regarding which model is most often used. But certain parties may require a deviation from the standard to meet their specific needs. A one-coach model may be beneficial because it saves on costs and doesn't suggest the partisan tone that a two-coach model may foster. But, in certain cases, especially those in which a party may suffer from mental health issues, substance abuse issues, domestic violence issues, etc., the two-coach model may be more effective.

Assuming that the facilitator is the mental health professional, early in the process, before the first full team meeting, she will help the clients identify their goals, interests, and concerns. It's important for each of them to understand the difference between a position and a goal or an interest. Focusing on positions rather than on interests limits settlement options. Identifying goals allows for more bargaining room and helps spouses understand that there's more than one way to resolve their divorce. It's important for the parties to prioritize their goals. Then the team can work to achieve each party's most important ones and compromise on their less important ones. Although people going through a divorce are in conflict, by focusing on interests rather than on positions, they're able to negotiate reasonably without using threats, intimidation, or ultimatums.

It is always surprising to me how often spouses in conflict, when they are able to focus on goals instead of positions, identify the very same interests and objectives, i.e. safety, security, privacy, protection of their relationships with their children and their friends, and similar honorable and highly principled motivations and concerns.

Once they have formulated them, the facilitator shares their goals with the other professionals on the team at the first teleconference, if not before. She routinely reminds them of those goals throughout the process. She may begin each full team meeting by reviewing them and ask each person to focus on the other party's goals. When one of them gets stuck on a position, or when the negotiations aren't proceeding as effectively as the team would like, the facilitator will remind them of their goals to help them brainstorm options. By negotiating interests rather than positions, parties are more likely to reach a mutually satisfying settlement agreement that they'll abide by going forward.

At the client's first meeting with the facilitator, she'll describe her role, clarifying how it differs from her role in therapy. In the collaborative process, the facilitator must *not* act as a therapist, even though the sessions may feel therapeutic. In a way, the collaborative process itself is the facilitator's client. But if one of them needs outside counseling, she can make outside referrals for counseling or other psychological intervention. If it is a one-coach model, the facilitator will explain that she is a neutral party.

She'll also explain that the importance of transparency, meaning that they must fully and candidly exchange information about the nature, extent, value of, and all developments affecting their income, assets, liabilities, and all other matters relevant to their divorce. She'll remind the clients that their conversations will be shared with the team.

The facilitator will also explain the concept of confidentiality. The team agrees to maintain the confidentiality of all collaborative communications relating to the subject matter of the case, whether before or after the institution of formal judicial proceedings, if any. But her meeting with the client isn't confidential and will be shared with the other team members.

She'll discuss the expectation that the clients will avoid offensive communications, destroying evidence, making financial decisions without the other parties' approval, etc.

The facilitator will discuss her retainer agreement and fees with the client, establishing the clients' responsibilities for her payment.

Most importantly, she'll interview and observe each client's dynamics. She'll make personal connections with the clients so that they are comfortable opening up to her. She'll discuss the history of the clients' relationship, specific concerns the client has, etc. She'll screen for issues that could derail negotiations, like power struggles, psychological problems, personality disorders, and addictions. In addition, she'll assess the couple's dynamics and communication skills. She'll determine whether domestic violence seems involved, and, if so, whether the collaboration can proceed, despite it.

The facilitator will then prepare a report to the other professionals outlining her interviews with the clients, explaining areas of concern and strategies for dealing with the specific type of client. She'll describe each client's readiness to proceed and any matters that may influence the pace and direction of the process.

Given that "heads up" from the facilitator, the other collaborative professionals will then work together to form a realistic plan of action.

The facilitator is particularly important at the first meeting, where she is probably the only professional with whom both parties have met. She'll have established a rapport with the parties and professionals, and will set the tone for the meetings. By helping the clients process their emotions, she'll know when best to take breaks or terminate meetings.

In addition, she'll consider the best seating arrangement for this team, whether it's more beneficial to have them sit across from one another, or side-by-side for a less adversarial climate. Once again, at the first meeting, the facilitator will review conduct expectations. As in all meetings, she'll actively listen, alert to verbal and non-verbal communications, and intervening when necessary.

After each meeting, the professionals will debrief. The facilitator should lead this session, praising the strengths of the team members, and constructively criticizing the weaknesses. She should lead them in considering whether the meeting goals were accomplished, whether the agenda was followed, whether the team communicated collaboratively and effectively, and whether the needs of the couple were addressed.

Most importantly, the team should discuss how to improve their effectiveness at the next meeting.

Between meetings, the facilitator may resolve the clients' disputes, act as a referral source, help to defuse or resolve conflicts, and act in any other way to keep the process moving swiftly. Not only is she a support system to the clients and professionals, but she can help with problem solving and creative thinking.

Because emotions often drive divorces, the facilitator is generally the most essential member of the collaborative team. Her interaction can change the tone in the room from an adversarial feeling when it is just two parties and their attorneys to a team dynamic. Clients are more likely to listen to a neutral facilitator than to an attorney whom they view as aligned with his or her client. For this reason, the facilitator is often the appropriate person to ask clients tough questions and elicit honest answers from them. They are invaluable members of the collaborative team.

Clients tell me all the time that their spouse is crazy or suffers from an addiction. This idea I suspect, helps them to explain to themselves why their marriages have gone into the toilet, *and* why the demise of the relationship isn't their fault. Often, there's a more straightforward explanation. Perhaps it's as simple as the fact that the parties neglected to work at growing together, have gone different directions over time, and it's too late to repair the rift. Or sometimes it's the fact that the grass has proven greener in the neighbor's yard.

But sometimes the client's spouse really *is* crazy. When that's the case, it's unfortunately true that the justice system is ill-equipped to offer the spouse the help that she really requires. And your client, who should have been her "next best friend" (as it is legally termed in some jurisdictions), is now her worst enemy, having sued her for divorce.

Even in such cases, a facilitator might be able to manage the meetings in such a way, perhaps with the help of a mental health specialist, a coach specifically for the mentally ill spouse, that the clients can reach agreement and that children can be protected from the worst of the maelstrom.

The Treasure

Carolyn Reitz was a pretty, young, Martha Stewart-type brunette. She often brought her 3½ year old son, JR, to our office. He was a cherubic-looking, devilish-acting boy, with gorgeous, bright blond, curly hair. I'll never forget the first time I met him.

I was quietly discussing legal matters with Carolyn as the precocious child ran in circles around my small office, jumping over the pottery gators and real conch shells decoratively placed, and knocking over chairs and files. He reminded me of my puppy, if I've left her home, when I return from a long day away from the house.

All of a sudden, he stopped and stated very loudly, "I have to poop now."

I exchanged glances with his mother. She looked a bit embarrassed, but gave me a nod indicating that we should ignore him.

We proceeded with our conversation, when the child nearly screamed, "I have to poop *now*." Again, the same look from his mother, so I attempted to proceed.

He jumped onto the desk and yelled, "Mommy, I have to poop *now!*"

Carolyn nervously giggled. "JR, get off of the desk this minute! I'll take you to the bathroom when I finish talking to the lady."

This concerned me. After all, there is nothing that I hate worse than a child defecating in my office. Nevertheless, I took my cue from Carolyn and continued talking. As I mentioned the word "divorce," the young devil child farted louder than I have ever heard. The sound reverberated around the room.

Carolyn remarked, "Well, I guess we know how he feels about that." Thankfully, she finally took him to the restroom.

JR wasn't the only interesting character in the family. She wanted to divorce her husband, Jake, because he suffered from severe mental illness. She believed it was the same manic depression that many of his relatives had.

Three weeks prior to our initial consultation, he'd moved out and into his parents' home, entertaining delusions that he'd found buried treasure in their backyard, booby-trapped with hematite to keep people away. He was obsessed with the number eight, dinosaur heads, turtles, and rocks. He dug holes all over their backyard. His behavior cycled quickly, from being extremely upset with Carolyn, to calling her trying to make small talk.

One morning prior to our initial consult, at approximately 3:00

a.m., he texted her.

> . . . I do have something that will change our lives forever. Im not hallucinating. Im perfecty sober. Weather you want to believe it or not I have definitely 100 percent without a shadow of a doubt found treasure. I wil come over right now to explain. I promise your from the botgom of my heart that we are about to be rich. Please please please belueve me. This is worth taking up for. No matter what you will be taken care of no matter what. I would like to work together on this one. Please im not pulling your chain. Please reply back if u get this. Im sure of treasure. 100000% please for once trust me. I also have logical explanation for my rash your irriatbility jrs rash. If im wrong u can use all this at court against me. Please trust me I will come ovef right now. Yku just need to here me out. I have at least one pound of gold in one piece If u dont hear me out u will never live it down. Im no asking u to look for holograms etc......i have hard undeniable proof U wilm not have to work ever again Let me know as soon u get this I would not bother u with this witg everything we are goinv through I can prove it without u havibg to look with one eye closed Jr will be staying home tomorrow. We need to figure out our next move Please just believe me for once.

He went on and on. Now, he said, he could explain why his memory was bad, why he had a rash, why they were unable to get pregnant again, why he suffered joint aches, stiff ankles, and shaky hands, and why she was having kidney troubles. He was concerned that they'd been exposed to high amounts of lead, and that was causing their health problems. He was "serious as a heart attack" that it all had to do with "pieces of eight."

He had found "a shit ton of treasure" in three different locations, including the parties' house. Alleging that a picture of the parties' yard from Google Earth showed a pattern that was on gold coins that he had found all over the yard, he asked Carolyn to keep the treasure private. He promised that she would never have to work again and swore that he wasn't crazy.

Jake was sure that a red mark near JR's eye was a rash caused by the hematite. There were faces of men in the trees at their home that had been affected by the hematite. He saw roman numerals on JR's bedroom door. These same "symbols" were on deflated balloons, garbage in the backyard, their sheets, rugs in the house, etc. By soaking rocks in vinegar and baking soda, he said that would clean them so that gold and silver would be visible.

Some of his imaginings were complex. A work of art coming up through his driveway could be seen if one wore three-dimensional glasses; he asked friends to put on the glasses and look at his driveway. The "art" was a picture of a pirate ship and a map leading to the treasure in their backyard, their neighbors' yard, and at Cypress Beach.

His ideations weren't limited to personal property. He repeatedly and unfoundedly accused her of cheating, being involved in a lesbian affair with her best friend, stealing from him, lying to him, abusing alcohol, recreationally taking his medications, suffering from a social networking addiction, and leaving guns around the house. He requested that she be checked for sexually transmitted diseases. He alleged that JR had a head injury which he attributed to her poor care because JR had a small red mark by his eye.

But he *also* believed this mark was caused by the hematite.

After my client told his parents about her husband's crazy texts, Jake's father took him to attend counseling sessions. The doctor prescribed medications for bipolar disorder, schizophrenia, ADHD, and anxiety. He recommended that Jake be committed if he failed to take his medications.

Jake tormented Carolyn by running around the outside of their home, knocking on all the doors and windows, and calling for JR, until Carolyn would call the police. While she was at work, he'd pick up JR from daycare so that she couldn't see him. He refused to attend family counseling and made timesharing exchanges impossible so that she'd miss time with their son. He threatened to unilaterally change JR's preschool and removed all of JR's clothing from the drawers in their home.

He attempted to frame her as a violent drunk by putting his shotgun on the ground at their home and taking a picture. He took pictures of an empty bottle of wine from the trash outside, cooking sherry, and a very nearly full bottle of red wine. He warned Carolyn that booze, guns, and depression do not mix and that he couldn't live with himself if he didn't tell someone about her "problem." He stole her wedding rings from their home. When she confronted him, he accused JR of taking them, even though JR could not reach the dish where she kept her rings and nobody else had been to the house.

After that, he accused her of pawning the rings to pay her attorney.

Following an emergency hearing at which the judge ordered supervised timesharing for Jake, he went to their home, threatening to break the window to gain access. Before the police arrived, he entered and removed several inconsequential items. A few days later, he broke in again and tore apart JR's bedroom because he was convinced Carolyn was hiding a dead body inside.

For several months, he refused to follow the court's orders regarding timesharing and exchanges, greatly reducing her time with her son. He refused to bring JR to weekend exchanges, keeping the child from her for entire weekends, and not even allowing JR to speak to her on the telephone.

He repeatedly picked up JR early, before Carolyn could arrive. During his timesharing, he refused to get JR to school, as ordered.

In an attempt to clear up confusion regarding the timesharing exchanges, the court issued another order regarding timesharing. He still ignored the order and when he had JR, he often turned off his phone completely and refused to answer Carolyn's e-mails.

Throughout Carolyn's battle with Jake, she was forced to battle with JR's daycare, as well. When she had advised the preschool that Jake shouldn't be allowed to drive with JR in his vehicle due to his current medications, the preschool informed her that it couldn't prevent him from taking JR without a court order.

So much for putting the safety of the child first.

When Carolyn received a temporary injunction granting her 100% temporary timesharing, she told the school that they couldn't release JR to Jake or to his mother. The administrators responded that they were "far too busy to watch one child." They claimed they didn't see that the injunction gave her "100% time sharing." On one occasion, the administrators informed her that she needed to come for JR immediately, or they'd let Jake's mother take him. Carolyn was forced to leave work to retrieve JR. When she arrived, the administrators had the temporary injunction in hand and said "Oh, we just found where it said you had custody."

Now for the icing on the crazy cake.

Jake began dating a teacher from JR's preschool, "Ms. Martha." When Carolyn warned her to watch out because the fact that she was dating Jake would come up in court, Ms. Martha told the school administration that Carolyn had threatened her.

A school administrator, Deborah Pratts-Smith, told Carolyn that what the teachers did on their own time was their business. A teacher wrote an unauthorized letter fraudulently alleging that JR attended the preschool for fewer hours than he really did.

The school threatened to send Carolyn, and not Jake, to a collection agency because of their past due balance, despite that it was owed by both of the parties. Then they refused to provide Carolyn with a payment history, despite the fact that they gave her a contract indicating that they were going to start assessing late fees to her, and not to him.

The administrators informed her that they would testify in court as to her "unprofessional behavior" and asserted that she was harassing them. Carolyn informed them they were violating the Florida Statutes as they related to high moral standards and the emotional wellbeing of a child for whom they had responsibility. They told her that they weren't responsible for employee behavior after 5:00 p.m. Carolyn asked whether morals and values ended at 5:00 p.m. They replied that they had no proof about what was going on, even though Ms. Martha admitted to it.

When the child care administrators told Carolyn that they'd take her to court, despite the fact that she was only trying to keep JR safe, she filed a complaint with Hillsborough County Child Care Licensing regarding the preschool's actions. They fought back by obtaining a temporary injunction against Carolyn, so that she could no longer go to the preschool, where the exchanges of JR had been ordered to occur.

When Carolyn asked Jake if they could change JR's preschool, he refused to respond. So she enrolled JR at a different preschool and told Jake. One hour after she dropped him off on his first day, Jake picked him up. Furthermore, despite the fact that she was unable to go to JR's preschool until the injunction hearing, Jake wouldn't agree that anyone except his family could attend the exchanges. Carolyn made arrangements for a friend to pick up JR, but Jake refused to allow it.

After two weeks, the injunction court denied the preschool's request for a final injunction against Carolyn. At the hearing, the bailiff had to tell one of the preschool workers to cover her breasts, another to stop chewing gum, and a third to turn off her phone, or the bailiff would remove them from the courtroom. During the hearing, Jake appeared to be very aggravated and left the courtroom three times. At the hearing, Jake called Carolyn and her friend "trash" and "drinking buddies." His father also made comments regarding Carolyn and her friend loud enough for them to hear.

At a family court hearing thereafter, Jake's counsel informed the court that Jake wasn't dating Ms. Martha, despite the fact that Ms. Martha admitted to it. His counsel assured the court that the preschool would send Carolyn a nice letter, telling her that she was welcome on the school's premises. She never received any such letter.

Instead, when Carolyn went to pick up JR, the administrators humiliated her by forcing her to face a wall while JR was escorted to the office. The owner refused to allow Carolyn past the front desk, so she was unable to walk him to his classroom, and JR sobbed as an administrator took him from her arms and carried him there.

It almost doesn't need saying that the family court granted our motion to allow Carolyn to change JR's school.

The court ordered a guardian *ad litem* and a timesharing facilitator. The facilitator recommended, and the court approved, that Jake was prohibited from sharing time with JR until he was under regular psychiatric care and could prove that he had been taking his medications for three months. It was finally the wake-up call that Jake needed. The one thing more important to Jake than his delusions was JR. The forced separation compelled Jake to follow his treatment plan. After he successfully achieved three months of counseling and medication, the timesharing facilitator requested that he be allowed to begin supervised timesharing with JR. After three more months of counseling, medication, and no delusional incidents, the final hearing was set. The facilitator recommended that Jake be allowed timesharing on alternating weekends as long as he continued his counseling and medication. That brief period without access to JR seemed to have scared him straight, and he has been a model co-parent since then.

When JR celebrated his eighth birthday, Carolyn was concerned that Jake's obsession with the number eight would resume. But so far, so good. She watches JR closely for signs that his father's mental illness has been passed down to him. He appears to be very normal, but Carolyn still cringes when he spends too much time digging in their sandbox or at the beach, concerned that he is searching for his father's buried treasure.

Life events can change people. A once-pleasant client can become a difficult and scary person. Whether it's due to a head injury or other physical maladies, post-traumatic stress disorder or untreated mental illness, or just the personality changes inflicted by unfortunate life woes, such alterations in behavior and temperament can be drastic and surprising.

Can a collaborative team work its magic in such a situation? It probably depends on the degree of the mental incapacity. While a collaborative team might have enabled Phil Candle to accept the resolution that was forced upon him, if ultimately all he really wanted was to indulge in the sparring, then, no, of course not.

The Plane Crash

Phil Candle was a former client, who returned to me with another litigation assignment. Eight years prior, I'd defended him and his wife, Susan, in a lawsuit brought against them in their former "laboratory business," as well as represented Phil in his post-dissolution-of-marriage matter, eliminating his alimony responsibility. Later I learned that the laboratory in question was owned by his son, but I wasn't aware of this until we parted ways.

The new matter involved litigation, ostensibly on behalf of a corporation owned by Susan, but of which Phil was plainly in charge. I met with her in my conference room, and he appeared telephonically.

Susan had hardly aged. Although she had to be 60, her hair

was pecan colored, with nary a silver hair in it. As far as I could tell she wore little makeup on her unlined face beside a light pink lip gloss. She wore two-inch pumps and a khaki suit, with her jacket over her arm; my office is a casual style and she relaxed, and crossed her legs at the conference table.

I greeted her warmly, reaching out with my right hand for a shake and then hugged her. "It's been a long time," I smiled. After we exchanged pleasantries and caught up a bit, we called Phil on her cell phone and put him on speaker.

With his former enthusiasm, he said, "Joryn, I want you for this matter!" In a nutshell, he planned to recover "surplus funds" neglected in the foreclosure process (i.e. those moneys paid by the winning purchaser over and above the amount owed to the foreclosing party) on behalf of the owners foreclosed out of the properties.

When he was finished describing the issues, I thought for a moment, and then voiced my concerns. "Phil, although this seems like a brilliant idea, your plan immediately raises the twin specters of 'champerty' and 'maintenance' in my mind, somewhat antiquated but still very viable torts. I'm not comfortable taking this case until I do some research. Do you agree that my associates and I may perform some legal research at our hourly rates?"

He begrudgingly agreed.

In retrospect, I believe he was surprised that that I perceived these concerns so quickly; such charges are rarely raised in this day and age, and most attorneys wouldn't have seen their implication. "My rates have climbed significantly since I last represented you, to $300/hour for me, and $150/hour for associates."

They agreed to pay for that research at the higher hourly rates. I didn't ask for a retainer because she was an old friend, they were both former clients, and I expected the research to require little time.

He indicated that he already had several attorneys representing the corporation in this endeavor, and, after our meeting, he e-mailed me the forms that they were allegedly using to do so, a Surplus Funds Agreement (a contract between Phil's corporation and the foreclosed party) and a Special Power of

Attorney (giving Phil's corporation the power to represent the foreclosed party in collecting the surplus funds).

After our meeting, I assigned my associate Anne to research the issues and to contact The Florida Bar Hotline regarding the ethical ramifications of our involvement. (I was also worried about "solicitation" issues, a far more common error made by attorneys who are overly zealous in their pursuit of prospective clients.)

According to Florida case law, the term "maintenance" refers to:

> . . . an officious intermeddling in a suit which in no way belongs to the intermeddler by maintaining or assisting either party to the action, with money or otherwise, to prosecute or defend it.

Although I often warn my clients that "anyone can sue anyone else for anything," they still run the risk of being held accountable for misusing the judicial system; one party may not lawfully suggest or induce another party to sue another.

The same court described "champerty":

> a form of maintenance wherein one will carry on a suit in which he has no subject-matter interest at his own expense or will aid in doing so in consideration of receiving, if successful, some part of the benefits discovered.

Champerty laws in Florida make it unlawful to contract for the sole or primary purpose of prosecuting litigation.

My associate and I quickly determined that I couldn't ethically represent them or the corporation. Anne met with Susan (Phil was not available on such short notice) to explain our concerns, both for them and for myself, and that we wouldn't represent them.

He expressed his displeasure with me for declining and accused me by e-mail of making him "look like an idiot to my guys in the field." During our meeting, he had apprised me of a recent plane crash he'd survived, without detailing the precise nature or extent of his consequent disabilities, so I responded to this e-mail mildly. "If you would like, Phil, I could contact the attorneys doing this work for you already, and discuss the issues."

In a somewhat rude response, he told me not to; I apparently had been intended to replace them. He didn't want them forewarned of his displeasure.

I acknowledged this instruction politely.

The following day, he wrote again, that the first e-mail was one that "should have been written and then thrown away." He apologized for not asking me to represent him sooner, although he also claimed "I thought you were strictly family law." This was odd as I had previously represented him in the commercial problem with his laboratory. In the second e-mail, he took a completely different tone, chatty and upbeat, suggesting that he might be proven wrong in his negative reaction to my assessment of the legality of the matter.

Once again, I responded politely. I invoiced Phil for our time, and received a check by return mail.

I heard nothing more from them until over a year later, when he e-mailed me "Girl, this is your lucky day." He wanted me to handle a new matter, saying, "I was pondering who would be best for this case. At the same time, Susan and I said "Joryn!!!!"

I was out of town, but I asked him to contact my assistant for an appointment. In the meantime, he e-mailed me more than once, because he wanted "to get you on record as my counsel."

It turned out that he wanted me to pursue a breach of contract matter over the sale of his laboratory.

I gave him our standard retainer agreement and explained again that I delegate work to my associate(s) when appropriate, as that is more cost-effective. Together, we determine the best strategy for our clients, in order to keep fees as low as possible.

He neither returned an executed agreement nor suggested any changes to it.

Instead, I billed him for seven months, and he never objected to the invoices, the amount of time spent on his file, or the hourly rate charged. After I assigned Anne to prepare a complaint for breach of contract, she researched and drafted it. She discussed the parties' positions with opposing counsel, and suggested mediation, a strategy to move the case closer to a successful resolution.

When we alerted him to this development, he was enraged that Anne had suggested it, although nowadays parties are almost always required to mediate at least once prior to going to trial. In any event, it was the right tactic here to obtain free discovery, to share each side's perspectives, and to move the parties closer to either settlement or trial.

Shortly thereafter, opposing counsel forwarded Phil's arguably threatening e-mail to his own client to me (among other things, "let's get it on!"), with a request that I instruct Phil to desist from contacting his clients directly.

In response to his strenuous complaint about Anne's suggesting mediation, I pointed out that I specifically reserve the right to assign work to associates as I see fit, that mediation made sense, and that he was holding a grudge against Anne because of her research in the earlier matter on champerty and maintenance.

I also forwarded opposing counsel's request to Phil, explaining it to him.

He replied, "Although I do not agree with mediation, I defer the decision to you." But he responded to opposing counsel's request in an agitated tone, clearly aggrieved by the other side's allegations. He demanded that we pursue the money he was owed, "plus $2M punitive." I chose not to answer, having learned that he might overreact initially, but, upon reflection, reach a different, more reasoned conclusion. So I let it rest.

In the meantime, we scheduled mediation. For several weeks, I heard nothing from him except one inquiry regarding status, with a note that he was in "no hurry" to discuss matters. Then, he complained to me that my associate had left him a telephone message while he was out of town. She theoretically should have known he was out of town. He said she'd misinformed him of the mediation date, although she *had* informed him of the first agreed-upon date immediately. It was later changed. He claimed that he only knew of the correct date because he "quite by accident" read her letter, informing him of the new date. He complained that she had referenced his matter therein as "Moyle v. Candle," rather than as "Candle v. Moyle." (We had yet to file an official complaint.)

He was very upset.

I responded respectfully, but expressed concern that he was "unhappy with our services. You seem to be looking for problems." Alerted to his evident mental and emotional problems, I proposed, "If you would prefer to transfer the case to another counsel, please don't hesitate to let me know." At the same time, I invited him to bring his account with us current.

Interestingly, despite that, when I had earlier reminded him to return our retainer agreement, he had said he had no idea where it was, this time he volunteered that it was signed. But he pretended to be unaware that he had already spent the $1,000 retainer, even though he had been sent an invoice, clearly showing that fact.

He instructed me to cancel mediation. When I asked "why?" his rationale was basically "Because I said so."

At this point, I requested that he pay an additional $1,000 refundable retainer fee, as well as the filing fee for his complaint.

He responded that we no longer represented him, and demanded a refund of his initial $1,000. He also notified opposing counsel that he had terminated our services. Then he telephoned my office requesting his file and a refund.

When I told him I would not only *not* refund his money, but that he owed us additional fees for the time already spent, he threatened to file a complaint with The Florida Bar.

> If this is a game . . . I will bring you to your knees. I am willing to walk away from this whole mess you caused if I have a one grand check in my hand tomorrow. No, I will not pick it up. Want to play it out? Let's frigging do it.

Obviously, this constituted blackmail, and I told him so.

Ten days later, I received another missive from him, claiming that his new attorney had called my office four times without a return call. Again, he threatened to grieve me with The Florida Bar. (My office had no record of such calls.) I suggested he give the attorney my extension, and stated he was "ignoring my request that you refrain from e-mailing me. Please be advised that I consider your continued use of my email address as harassment."

Nevertheless, he persisted in e-mailing and even visited my

office to personally harass me. (I didn't come to the door, but my assistant was a bit shaken by her encounter with him.) By now, he had received notice from my collection agency, and he informed me that his wife had been recently diagnosed with Stage IIIB ovarian cancer. He described her condition in macabre detail and included color photographs of the diseased ovary and a tumor on her colon. According to him, her possible five-year survival rate was less than five percent, although he hadn't shared that with her!

"Susan doesn't stand a chance in hell but only her doctors and I know that. No one in the family knows this but me." Yet, oddly, he felt compelled to send this information, along with the gruesome photos, to me, the attorney he had fired, when I had specifically requested that he stop e-mailing me. Clearly an intimidation ploy, but I responded courteously.

He sent a cascade of e-mails. He threatened to report me to The St. Pete Times. He went on "obviously this now goes well beyond the Bar. You may elect to be a crook or elect to mess with me, but you can't elect to be a crook AND mess with me." He sent another copy of his demand for payment.

> I again attach it and make demand for that refund. Should this be amenable to you, I take no pleasure in grieving the Bar, but justice must be served. I am willing to drop the entire matter and write it off to experience if you are willing to return my $1,000.

Later, he sent yet another harassing note, "I would strongly advise you to furnish me with explanations and they'd better be damned good and they'd better be soon." On the same date, he copied me on an e-mail to the St. Pete Times, complaining "the situation has exacerbated to the extent that I believe public expose is indicated." He made good on his threat to grieve me with The Florida Bar. And, of course, he vowed to sue me for malpractice.

> I want you to anguish as Susan and I have. I would love to visit you in prison but I fear that won't happen. I'll settle for disbarment.

His next e-mail demanded that I have a copy of my response to his complaint to The Florida Bar "in my hands" by the date of the deadline to respond.

In one e-mail, he identified the crux of the problem. "I am so furious with you that I cannot think rationally." He admitted, "I'm a very creative and, at the moment, vindictive person," and a man who has "brain damage from a plane crash."

I wished he had informed me of the specific nature of his disability before I agreed to perform legal services for him.

During this time, I arrived at the office one day to discover that someone had thrown a baseball through my $7,000 sign out front. I arranged to replace it.

Three different times, I instructed my business operations manager to place Phil's e-mail address on the "blocked senders" list. Nevertheless, I continued to receive his intimidating and threatening e-mails. He apparently bypassed my strategy by changing his e-mail address.

Unfortunately, as he had so clearly demonstrated, he was unable to control his frustration and anger, leaving me concerned that he would take it out on the closest possible target. His behavior made me fear that I would be one of those victims we hear so much about, "the lawyer who the client shot." Therefore, I petitioned for a domestic violence injunction against him, and the court granted it for a year.

Immediately after the court granted it, Phil moved to modify it. Although it specified that he "shall not directly or indirectly contact Petitioner [me] in person, by mail, e-mail, fax . . . ," he faxed and mailed this motion directly to me. He alleged that he was represented by an attorney whom he never actually retained. His motion was baseless and the court denied it.

Six weeks later, I was compelled to move for contempt against him because he refused to turn his firearms over to the sheriff, as required by the injunction. In court again, the judge ordered him to relinquish possession of all firearms, and he finally did so.

About a month prior to the termination of the injunction, Phil sent me an "invoice" for $238,040, charging me for work that he claimed to have performed in my actions against him. He addressed the envelope in which the "invoice" was mailed to "The Law Offices of Joryn Jenkins, a State of Florida Illegal Entity." He also sent my associate an e-mail, inviting her to join MySpace.

I moved to extend the term of the injunction. During the week prior to the hearing, Phil moved to recuse the judge in a seven-page written diatribe, making derogatory statements about me and Anne, specifically mentioning my step-daughter (who lived with me) and her mother, and insulting the court. He mentioned the brain damage that he had suffered, going on to state:

> Joryn Jenkins is a criminal. Ironically, I am the one whose record is besmirched and treated as a criminal in court. I make the statement about Jenkins without any fear of a libel suit. I will willingly state it publicly. I intend to. The unsuspecting public must be protected from this woman . . . . I am not a violent person, but there are such in this world. One day Jenkins is going to make the mistake of attempting to extort them and find that a piece of paper called an injunction will provide her no protection.

The judge denied his recusal motion and granted my request for an extension of the injunction for another year. That same day, Phil moved to modify the injunction. I moved to suspend his concealed weapons license, and he failed to attend the hearing on that, so the judge ruled in our favor.

I filed a collection suit for breach of contract against him, and received a judgment for the full amount he owed my firm.

One day, I received a telephone call from a woman who claimed to be his ex-girlfriend. After several cautious calls and a detailed explanation of her situation, I began to believe this woman, who claimed to have broken up with him when she discovered he was already married and had been during their long-term affair. Apparently, he wouldn't take her "no" for an answer and continued to visit her farm two hours north of Tampa to practice shooting his guns. She explained that she was pleasant to him, because she was afraid of his emotional instability. She confirmed that it was Phil who had thrown the baseball through my sign.

She contacted me periodically to inform me about his actions and threats against me. He never knew that his lover was in cahoots with me! What a fitting turn of events. Eventually her calls were fewer and farther in between.

Now, five years later, Susan is still alive, as far as I know, and I wonder if she was ever ill. Before my injunction expired, she brought a check to my office for the full amount that Phil owed us. It was quite the unexpected surprise.

More often than you might think, divorce is caused by a significant change in one spouse's personality or behavior that the other is simply unequipped to handle. Sometimes it's addiction to painkillers, gambling, recreational drugs, or internet pornography. Sometimes mental illness emerges, like manic depression, schizophrenia, multiple-personality syndrome, or even some combination thereof.

Addiction or illness complicates the traditional courtroom divorce, because it doesn't involve a mental health professional who is there to assist the handicapped person in dealing with the divorce issues. Without this help, that party's ability to participate meaningfully in the judicial process is compromised.

The Aliens

Divorce attorneys think we've heard it all. Then, Ross Marchesi strode through my front door.

Right from the get-go, he was always disheveled, with long, wiry hair, a greasy complexion, and loose-fitting, faded clothing. A tall, rangy man, he left a stale, lingering odor in every room. His crazy eyes darted around the room, only settling on an object momentarily before flitting off to focus on another. I could feel his anxious energy as soon as I entered a room where he was. He'd sit briefly, stand, and then pace. He always fidgeted with his hands, and occasionally beamed the headlights of those eyes on me.

He brought his friend, Drew Foster, for our initial consultation.

Marchesi insisted that we consult with him when determining case strategy. Foster, a disbarred attorney, had interesting views on maintaining ethics and professionalism. Needless to say, I was skeptical about his legal opinions.

Foster was smarmy. Each time he departed, I felt the need to check my belongings to ensure that they were all still there. Like Marchesi, he was unkempt, wearing clothing that was too small on his bloated body. One side of his shirt would be un-tucked while his pants flapped around his ankles. A trace of his previous meal, usually what might have been a meatball hoagie or Philly cheesesteak, typically adorned his face or clothes.

I went through my general opening dialogue for initial consultations, and then asked Marchesi what had brought him to our office. In the brief glance he gave me before his bloodshot eyes whizzed away, his eyeballs grew large, almost popping out of his head. "My wife is wackadoo," and he twirled his finger around his ear, giving me the universal sign for insanity.

Ross explained that his wife was involved with a cult-like organization called *Ramtha School of Enlightenment*. As far as I could determine, *Ramtha* is a for-profit corporation with no religious tax exemption with the IRS.

After Wackadoo attended several *Ramtha* events a year earlier, her behavior radically changed after that. She developed unfounded phobias and grandiose beliefs. She said that she communicated with aliens from other planets, and became extremely antagonistic to Marchesi and to others.

She believed that, at 4:44 a.m. on many mornings, she "channeled" aliens. She arose at 4:30 each day to attend these meetings and kept a "dream journal" in which she recorded "automatic writings where she connected with higher intelligence."

I've never read anything as fascinating as Wackadoo's dream journals. Each time she "channeled" a different alien, her manner of speaking and handwriting both changed.

Wackadoo allegedly spoke to them, as well, and Marchesi had the audio records to prove it! However, it was difficult to distinguish anything more than babbling and angry ranting.

Before we filed Marchesi's divorce petition, she was detained for mental health evaluation pursuant to the Baker Act. According to the psychological evaluation the doctors performed on her then, prior to our initial consultation, his wife had "anger management problems, low stress tolerance, and troubled emotional and psychological functioning." "Without help," the evaluator had said, "the prognosis is not good."

People have the right to believe what they want. However, in this case, an eight-year-old son, Arie, was involved. I can't imagine the consequences he'd have faced had he ever shared his mother's peculiar beliefs with his friends.

She was convinced that the end of the world was coming. Soon. She believed that the world as we know it would experience dramatic changes in the near future from natural catastrophes, economic collapse, and alien invasion from outer space. Okay, she was right about the economic collapse and natural catastrophes, but *I* still think she's crazy.

She said that the aliens had advised her to separate from her husband and to inform Arie about them. She told Arie this, as well as that the U.S. Government leaks gas from airplanes to control population growth and that these gases are referred to as "chem-trails."

Needless to say, this frightened the young boy.

Wackadoo believed that, when the world ends due to massive flooding, the only safe place will be in Colorado at the highest elevation. Why Colorado I have no idea; perhaps the aliens like to ski?

According to Joseph Szimhart, an expert in cult information and a cult exit counselor, "these phobias or false beliefs are so strong that new members will want to pack up everything and move closer to a "safe" area as designated by the Ramtha." Ramtha is an unhealthy social and intellectual environment for children because it induces false fears and teaches pseudo-science rather than reality.

According to Sue Brewer, a licensed social worker who was also familiar with Wackadoo's writings,

> While channeling and other new age philosophies are often used to enhance one's feeling of well-being

and inspire a person to feel empowered, messages of harm and doom which encourage people to move their families, stockpile arms, and/or break up their relationships may denote a basic instability of the individual and warrant further psychological or psychiatric evaluation.

Marchesi told me that his wife was physically and sexually abused as a child by her grandfather, and had been raped by him. In addition, she traumatically watched her father die, and was physically abused with "extreme punishment" by her mother. If true, it helps explain her susceptibility to Ramtha's irrational beliefs.

Because her mother, Sandy Presley, and her siblings, Chad and Anne Dean, shared the same beliefs, they encouraged her. As perpetuators of this cult, her family enabled, nurtured, and protected her mental instability.

As far as I could tell, my client was rightfully concerned that Wackadoo or her equally nutty family would punish Arie with the same kind of "extreme physical punishment" that they had endured as children. Marchesi was also worried that she would take Arie to Colorado.

Recently, she had stated in a correspondence to Michael Knight, another member of Ramtha and the director and editor of "Contact Has Begun," that she planned to move with Arie, probably to Colorado. She drew pictures of her dreams as well, and one picture displayed herself in Colorado, appearing god-like.

At the emergency hearing on our motion for temporary custody, we relied on a prior case that was similar to Marchesi's. In that case, the court had accepted the husband's testimony that his wife might move to another country and that there was danger of physical abuse. The court had therefore limited his wife to supervised visitation with their child.

The trial court believed the risk was real. Therefore, when the wife appealed, the appellate court was unable to say that the trial court had abused its discretion, but it did warn:

... the severity of this limitation on this parent/child

relationship is such that it should be subject to reconsideration by the trial court as circumstances warrant, including the question whether, on balance, some less drastic remedy would restrict the mother's ability to remove the child to Columbia.

Similarly, we argued that Marchesi's legitimate fear that Wackadoo would remove Arie to Colorado and her written plan to move with him was "some evidence." This, coupled with her present mental state, as well as the negative effect that her beliefs and actions might have on the child, warranted that her visitation be supervised until circumstances justified the court's reconsideration.

A pragmatic, down-to-earth judge I had known for years presided over the emergency temporary relief hearing. Stan Garson, who represented Wackadoo, argued that everyone is entitled to their beliefs, no matter how bizarre. But he forgot to consider the best interests of the child, Arie.

The ever-skeptical Judge Pinon gave Marchesi temporary primary residential responsibility of Arie and temporary exclusive use and possession of the home. She ordered supervised visits and appointed another lawyer (a volunteer) to be Arie's guardian *ad litem*. She ordered that the GAL interview Arie and the parties and witnesses, and recommend whether visits should be supervised and whether any restrictions should be placed on his visits with his mother. Following this, the parties would return to court for a continued temporary relief hearing.

Needless to say, Marchesi was elated.

Unfortunately for him, and in keeping with the theme of his case, the GAL was extremely eccentric. She resembled a hippy, often wearing long, flowing, floral dresses and sandals. She had long, stringy hair. She spoke in a dreamy tone, often gazing into the distance. And she vehemently supported Wackadoo's right to believe as she wished.

When we returned for the continued hearing, the GAL recommended that Wackadoo's timesharing *not* be supervised. In an ironic twist fitting for such a case, she accused Marchesi of *alienating* Wackadoo from Arie.

Thankfully, Judge Pinon remained skeptical and left the supervised visitation in place. Our representation of Marchesi ended soon thereafter, when he was unable to afford our services. We continue to hope that Arie is safe.

Chapter Seven

One-Coach Versus Two-Coach Model

The mental health professional plays an important role, if not *the* most critical role in the collaborative process. The MHP may serve either as a neutral facilitator or as a specific client's coach. Either way, the mental health professional brings a specific skill set to the collaborative team that assists the entire team in establishing an atmosphere of cooperation, reasonableness, respect, and trust. What are the differences between the one-coach model and the two-coach prototype?

In a one-coach model, the MHP facilitator prepares the agendas, runs the meetings, watches the time, keeps the team on track, and helps to maximize the process and outcomes. Throughout the process, he may assist the clients in negotiation and will likely teach them problem-solving skills and effective communication skills. He may employ various strategies to enhance the collaborative team members' effectiveness.

If there are children involved, he will likely assist the clients in recognizing and coordinating their respective parenting styles to enhance their future co-parenting relationship. If a child specialist is not a member of the team, the facilitator will help the clients with their parenting plan.

Regardless of whether there are children involved, the facilitator plays a crucial role because he assists the clients in achieving acceptable outcomes, identifying and taking into consideration their expressed goals, interests, and concerns.

Because the facilitator is trained in human behavior, communication skills, personalities, etc., he is more able than the other professionals to defuse destructive situations and prevent progress-halting situations. He monitors the emotional temperature of the room and watches for signs of disturbance in the participants or team members. He calls for a break if tension mounts unacceptably, and asks for clarification if a statement is ambiguous or confusing.

He does not wear his therapist's hat during the collaborative process, and his conversations with the clients are not confidential. He provides important information to the rest of the team about how best to conduct meetings and ultimately reach agreement. If there is a personality issue, the facilitator may refer the client to a therapist or other specialist for help or support. In the one-coach model, neutrality cannot be compromised. The neutral coach will work between the two participants, maintaining neutrality by being transparent between them. He will be responsible for meeting preparation and other administrative duties. He will generally attend all collaborative full team meetings.

By contrast to the one coach model, with two, each client has her own coach with whom she meets individually. Although the coaches may not run the meetings (the financial professional does that), they have many of the same responsibilities as in the one-coach model: they identify and assess their client's interests; provide education about communication and parenting; and manage their client's emotions. They don't act as therapists, and their communications aren't confidential, although they may make referrals to other professionals.. Each will generally do more one-on-one work with clients and have the opportunity to know the client in more depth. She'll share opinions and ideas with the other coach on the case, attend fewer full team meetings and will have less administrative responsibilities.

Thus, depending on whether the collaborative team opts for a one-coach or two-coach model, the MHP may or may not act as a neutral professional. Each collaborative community has its own protocols regarding which model is more comfortable. But certain participants may require a different choice to meet their specific needs. While a one-coach model may be beneficial because clients believe they will save on costs, it may not foster the more oppositional tone that the two-coach, two-lawyer model seems to suggest.

However, in certain cases, especially those in which a client may suffer from mental health issues, substance abuse issues, domestic violence issues, etc., a two-coach model may prove more effective.

If offered the choice, many clients will choose a one-coach model, assuming that it will be less expensive. It can be very difficult to convince participants to hire an entire collaborative team, when they look at the combined hourly rates of the professionals. Adding one more may be more costly than the clients believe they can handle. However, if the two-coach model is the more appropriate and effective model for the specific participants, it may ultimately be *less* expensive because the clients may be able to resolve their matters more quickly and with fewer full team meetings.

In reality, the cost differences between the two models are fairly negligible because the number of coaching sessions is relatively the same. In fact, the end cost of the process usually depends on the participants, rather than on the number of coaches. If clients prepare their homework, are organized and on-time for meetings, cooperate with the team, avoid arguing over insignificant matters, actively participate in meetings, and negotiate their interests rather than their positions, their divorce will cost less, regardless of the number of coaches.

For high conflict couples, a two-coach model may be more appropriate. These cases often involve personality disorders, mental illness, substance abuse, and/or domestic violence. In cases involving one of the first three issues, it may be more effective for the clients to each have a non-neutral coach who can and will be more involved with the client and who will take a more hands-on approach.

Cases involving domestic violence, on the other hand, usually involve a power imbalance. A one-coach model may not meet the needs of these couples because a neutral coach won't be as able to effectively stand up for rights of the domestic violence victim and still remain neutral. It's important for each person to have his or her own advocate when there's disproportionate power, or the aggressor may control the victim, leading to an unjust settlement, if one is even reached.

In any of these situations, it may be difficult at the outset to spot these high conflict cases because people tend, at least initially, to present their best selves.

As with anything, there are advantages and disadvantages to both models. An advantage of the one-coach model is that the coach attends every meeting, so she is completely informed of the issues, concerns, status, etc. Also, because the coach knows both clients, there is less chance of alignment. Furthermore, some individuals are resistant to coaching or anything they view as similar to therapy. However, in a one-coach model, it may be easier to get such a person to participate because she won't view the coach as her own coach, just as another member of the team. She'll see it as a practice norm, and she'll be coached regardless because the coach attends every meeting. Finally, calendaring meetings may be easier because there is one less professional to schedule.

A disadvantage to the one-coach model is that the mental health facilitator has more of an administrative function and less of a supportive role. Moreover, the neutral coach doesn't have the support and reflections of the other coach on the case. Argument and hostility are more easily handled by two professionals, who have established a supportive relationship with each client in advance.

There are several advantages to the two-coach model. The participants may feel stronger and more comfortable with their own coaches because they each have the support of a mental health advocate. Each coach will be able to pay more attention to his or her client. This is especially important in cases involving power imbalances, allowing participants to more comfortably communicate with one another.

Two coaches working together may be more successful at managing the clients' high emotions. They'll confer with one another, sharing each client's goals and concerns, and working together to determine how to reach the best resolution for both participants. They'll benefit from the skills, education, and insight of both of the coaches. The coaches will each support his or her client's lawyer, which may be necessary when dealing with especially difficult clients.

However, there may be disadvantages to this model. When each client has his own lawyer and his own coach, they might not be as able to work with the entire team, viewing it as a more hostile "us against them" environment. If the coaches align themselves with their or compete with each other, it creates difficulties. Depending on their training and education, they may have different theoretical orientations, which also could create issues. Because the coaches aren't present at every meeting between the other coach and other client, they may have a less complete picture than a one-coach team has. Additionally, scheduling four professionals is challenging enough, and adding one more makes it more difficult.

Although there are advantages and disadvantages to both models, most cases that are appropriate for collaborative practice will be successful using either. When considering which to use, discuss the specific needs of both you and your spouse with your attorney. Consider the general practice in your community. But also be open to trying a different archetype, especially if your purposes would be better served under a different model than the one with which your attorney is most comfortable.

Chapter Eight

The Financial Professional

The neutral financial professional (often referenced as the "FP") plays an important role in the collaborative process, whether he is the facilitator in the "two-coach model" or the FP in the "one-coach model." Unlike his persona in a litigated courtroom case in which both parties may hire CPAs to battle it out against one another, in a collaborative case, the FP acts as a neutral for both clients. The obvious benefit is that the clients save money by only retaining one FP and sharing the cost.

But that savings isn't a straight 50% of the amount that two experts would cost. When an expert prepares for trial, he also prepares to defend his opinion, and helps the trial attorney attack the other expert's reasoning and opinion. Although sometimes much more, on average, this added responsibility doubles the expense of the simple preparation of an opinion.

He's essential, even if the clients don't have high incomes or extensive assets. In some divorces, the biggest challenge is divvying up the debt. These days, whether to file a joint petition for bankruptcy protection *before* obtaining the divorce is often an issue that clients should consider — one far easier to do in a collaborative setting.

A financial professional will know best how to maximize the income and assets that the clients do have. He facilitates gathering financial information and problem-solving for everyone. Additionally, an FP may help clients identify their financial goals, interests, and concerns. He'll likely prepare an inventory of the clients' assets and liabilities. He may help the clients to develop budgets and to better understand the financial issues and options for property valuation. He may assist the attorneys and clients to address separate property and reimbursement claim issues. He will likely help the clients to develop, evaluate, and negotiate options for their financial settlement.

The FP will help the clients gather and organize their financial information. In a litigated divorce, the attorneys are generally responsible for organizing and reviewing the mandatory discovery. However, in the collaborative process, the FP, who is better trained in financial matters and who generally bills at a lower hourly rate than the attorneys do, will prepare the clients' joint mandatory discovery response.

In a litigated case, the attorney usually presides over any conferences between the client and the expert, and often meets with the expert outside the client's presence. In most collaborative communities, any meeting between the FP and the client takes place without the need for the attorney's attendance. Obviously, this is another huge cost savings to the collaborative client.

Because the clients pledge transparency, fully and candidly exchanging information of the nature, extent, value of, and all developments affecting their income, assets, liabilities, and all other relevant matters, costs are lowered. The clients avoid wasting time and money paying their attorneys to play litigation games to avoid fully disclosing financial information.

The information exchanged during the FP's meetings with the clients is not confidential with respect to the collaborative team; it will be shared with the other team members.

However, while the clients are transparent as to the team, the team agrees to maintain the confidentiality *within the team* of all collaborative communications relating to the subject matter of the case, whether before or after the institution of formal judicial proceedings, if any. The clients also agree to keep as much of their financial information confidential as the court will allow. (Remember the requisite final step in *any* divorce is still to get that final judgment of dissolution of marriage from a judge.) The amount of privacy allowed is based on what the individual judge or venue law requires, but here, in Florida, the team aims to file what we call "naked" financial affidavits, and many judges permit it. These are affidavits with the bare minimum of identification information that state that the fully completed versions (containing the personal financial information) have been exchanged by the clients. They attest that the clients have each placed the other's original affidavit in a secure location for future use, if needed.

We also avoid filing marital settlement agreements so that the information disclosed in these documents likewise doesn't become available to the public. By contrast, in the vast majority of litigated divorces, highly detailed marital settlement agreements are filed in the public court file for all to see.

The FP must appear neutral to the clients in his oral and written communications. Often, he'll spend more time with one client or the other because she is the one who has more of the financial information or because she is ignorant of the finances and requires more in the way of explanation. If so, the FP should explain to the clients why more time is being spent with one or the other, without making that client feel insecure.

The FP must only work within the scope of his engagement during the collaborative process. If the scope of engagement increases or decreases, the changes should be made in writing and approved by the team.

While engaged in the process, the FP may not solicit the clients for services outside the scope of engagement. However, after the process, the FP may perform services for the clients if requested by a client during the engagement, if the FP is able to remain neutral, if it is disclosed to the team, and if both clients consent to it after disclosure.

Early in the process, the clients may have less contact with the FP compared to the facilitator and their attorneys. (See Chapter Six for a discussion of the initial responsibilities of the facilitator in the collaborative process.) If the attorneys and clients agree that the clients should be involved in choosing the neutrals, the clients may briefly interview potential FPs. They'll discuss their fees and the scope of their work. They'll assess FPs based on resumes, personality types, and the clients' perceived needs. To avoid

115

overwhelming the clients early in the process, the FP may wait until after the first full team meeting to begin dialogues with the clients about financial disclosures, completion of financial affidavits, and their desires for the distribution of the assets and liabilities.

At that point, the FP will meet with each client one-on-one to identify their assets and liabilities and determine which client will provide which documents regarding sources of income and records of earnings. He'll discuss possible valuation dates, methods of valuation, and the need for appraisals.

Once he has the information, he'll organize it in a manner that will best facilitate settlement. He may assist the clients in obtaining values for their assets. He may recommend appraisers. He may educate the clients on financial and tax matters, if these are in his area of expertise. He may recommend additional neutral professionals, if, in his judgment, the clients' financial picture requires more specialized help. He will assist the clients in crafting financial scenarios for settlement.

An FP (and the other professionals, too, for similar cause) may withdraw from the process for the following reasons:

✓ if a client attempts to limit the scope of the FP's representation;
✓ if a client withholds information;
✓ if a client or attorney attempts to work outside the collaborative protocols;
✓ if there are threats of litigation, coercion, or intimidation;
✓ if the clients refuse to pay the FP;
✓ for problematic communications with a client or attorney; or
✓ for any other reason outlined in the FP's retainer agreement or the collaborative participation agreement.

If an FP does withdraw, he must give the team written notice, he must aid his successor FP, and he must make all relevant documents accessible to the team, though his work product is not admissible in court.

The FP is an integral part of every collaborative team. And

because he is neutral, the clients benefit from reduced expert fees, as well as from having a representative who is looking after both of their interests, rather than those of just one of them.

In litigation, to "sandbag" someone (always the opposing party) is a term of art, and its practice is an art form. In various kinds of adversarial settings, the term "to sandbag" means to purposely place oneself in an apparently weaker position to convey deceptively that one is less skilled than one truly is. Nothing is transparent, for as long as that is possible. And it's usually your forensic CPA who will find the missing information for your client. But not always. As the following account demonstrates.

The Smoking Gun

Don't get me wrong; I *love* trial work. Some parties will never be transparent, and it's so much fun to pit your wits against theirs! I once represented a husband and wife who had recently purchased a truck stop restaurant just off the interstate. The exit practically chuted customers to their front door. But a couple of years later, the Department of Transportation closed the exit.

My clients were convinced that the prior owners knew this was to happen. They believed that these folks, who had sold them the truck stop, were fully aware of the pending closure.

Their reasoning made sense. After all, a great deal of planning precedes shutting down a federal interstate highway exit. The restaurant was highly profitable and the prior owners were not yet retirement age.

We filed a complaint in state court. State law warns *caveat emptor*, "let the buyer beware," when it comes to purchasing commercial real estate, but *not* if there's outright fraud.

Discovery was slow going. It was like slogging through a marshy bog where mud threatened to suck the very boots off our feet. We struggled to get relevant documents from anyone, including the Department of Transportation. I finally scheduled the deposition of "the person with knowledge of" closing down the exit. I set his deposition *duces tecum*. This required him to produce any and all documents that had anything at all to do with the decision.

My clients were actively involved. Our scheduled deposition took place at the dilapidated three-story office building that housed the Department of Transportation. When I appeared to depose Eric Blackstone, its designated representative, Carmen met me in the second-floor lobby. At a mere five feet tall, she had the dark hair and olive complexion that I always associated with an Italian heritage. "Augie is working," she explained. She carried a zippered padfolio stuffed with loose papers a quarter-inch thick. I recognized the paperwork. She brought it to every appointment. It was her file on the lawsuit.

When we announced ourselves to the matronly grey-haired woman manning the front desk, she asked, "Are you expected?" We were. She made a phone call using a quiet voice. After she hung up, she directed us to chairs. "You can wait over there until someone can come down to take you up."

I asked, "Is our court reporter here yet?"

"Yes, indeed. She's already set up in the conference room."

The green vinyl chairs were uncomfortable, but we had little choice. Minutes passed while my client and I discussed additional questions that she wanted me to ask Mr. Blackstone.

The elevator chimed again. When its doors slid open, it revealed Seth Salcines, my opposing counsel, briefcase in hand. He caught my eye, and, instead of approaching the receptionist, he strode over to us with his right hand extended. I stood and shook it.

When we were ushered into the conference room, Mr. Blackstone was already seated. I was surprised that he had no paperwork of any kind in front of him.

I immediately asked whether he had brought any documents. He smiled as he gestured behind him, through the glass wall of the conference room, to a wall of standard four-drawer file cabinets. "They're full of the documents that you identified in your request."

"Do we have your permission to look through those documents?"

"Yes, you can help yourself."

There were actually three filing cabinets full of documents responsive to our inquiry. I selected one, Carmen took one, and that left Seth with the third. Blackstone left us to our own devices, handing us each a pad of post-it notes. "Just pull out the files and put a sticky note on anything you want a copy of. I'll be back in an hour."

Halfway through mine, hands grimy with dust mites, I discovered "the smoking gun." It was a form letter, but signed in blue ink and addressed to the DOT, in which the petitioner had handwritten her specific reason (in blue again) requesting that the DOT reconsider closing down the exit, "because it will force my restaurant out of business."

The request had been executed by the seller's wife.

The entire manila file in which the petition was buried was filled with similar entreaties. Each one came from business owners with locations at the erstwhile interstate exit. Two of them had been signed by the seller himself, and there was even one executed by the seller's son. Each detailed the reasons that closing the exit would hurt their restaurant business.

My breath caught in my throat. I grew up with *Perry Mason*. I had heard of the proverbial "smoking gun," but I had never expected to find one. To experience it. But that's exactly what this was.

Seth's parting comment to me was "I'm just glad that I wasn't the one to find them. I don't know what I would have done. I would hope that I would have disclosed them to you, but who the hell knows . . . ."

We settled the case early the next week.

Chapter Nine

Building Effective Collaborative Teams

The team is a crucial component of collaborative practice. Divorce is complex, complicated by many emotional and financial issues. The differing views of team members can offer the spouses new options, as well as allow the child's voice to be heard, without actually involving the child in the stressful process. Each team member uses his best skills rather than stretching himself to be *everything* for the client. Financial resources are maximized because the team spends time creating solutions rather than causing the other side problems, as in the traditional courtroom paradigm.

Further, they immediately address emotional issues that could inhibit the process. And neutrals who bill at lower hourly rates each utilize his or her particular expertise to more effectively resolve specific issues.

Effective team members are honest and respectful, supportive, willing to listen and problem solve, trusting, caring, helpful, and open. (They sound like boy scouts, don't they?) Valuable collaborative team members, including the clients, are responsible to the others to identify and resolve issues utilizing their varying perspectives.

The first step to building an effective team is to develop good relationships with other collaborative professionals in your community. Join a local practice group. Attend collaborative trainings. Volunteer for practice group committees. When a new member joins your practice group, take her out to lunch and get to know her socially. Maintain these relationships by meeting with other collaborative professionals often. People tend to suggest individuals with whom they have good personal relationships. And people tend to work better with those to whom they feel close. With friends.

To build the best team possible, consider administering personality tests to potential members. Avoid assembling people with the same personality type. Variety is crucial, especially considering the differing roles that each member plays. Lawyers tend to be highly autonomous and to share many personality traits that distinguish them from the general public. The Caliper Profile is a well-respected scientific instrument for in-depth personality assessment and job matching. It measures over 25 personality traits that relate to job performance.[2]

They tend to score very highly in "skepticism"; they're more skeptical, cynical, judgmental, questioning, argumentative, and self-protective than members of the general populace. While these traits benefit a trial attorney, they may hinder a collaborator, who must be more trusting and accepting.

Attorneys also tend to score very highly on the "urgency" scale. Their tendency to impatience makes them push for tasks to be performed and results to be accomplished immediately, unaware that they move more quickly than most people. But, if made aware of this, many attorneys can learn to be more patient.

This latter skill benefits a collaborative attorney, who can only proceed as quickly as the slowest member of the team. Often at least one party needs time to process, and rushing him will only cause him to shut down or react in other destructive ways. Furthermore, urgent people tend to be poor listeners, and developing good active listening skills is crucial in successful collaborative work.

Lawyers also tend to score low in "sociability," which may not bode well, as it measures an individual's desire to interact with people, especially for initiating new connections. Many lawyers may prefer focusing on individualistic loner-type tasks, like

---

[2] "Herding Cats: The Lawyers Personality Revealed," Managing Partner Forum: Advancing the Business of Law, Dr. Larry Richard.

research and writing, rather than the teamwork skills necessary for collaborative practice.

Additionally, typically, attorneys score low in "resilience" or "ego strength," demonstrating defensiveness or hypersensitivity to criticism. An important part of the process is the post-meeting debrief, in which the professionals highlight and critique each other's various strengths and weaknesses. Some lawyers may not be able to handle negative feedback as well as other team members. That doesn't mean that you should avoid constructively criticizing them, but perhaps be gentler as you do.

Moreover, attorneys score high in "autonomy." This means that the facilitator should be especially aware that the lawyers may resist being managed.

Many attributes that distinguish lawyers from the general population are negative. They're more likely to have a low interest in people, emotional concerns, and interpersonal matters. They're less humanitarian, colder, and more quarrelsome. Generally extroverted and social, they exhibit more masculine qualities like argumentativeness, competitiveness, aggression, and dominance. Because of their high need for achievement based on an external or internal standard of excellence, they tend to focus on the economic bottom line rather than on intangible concerns. They're more likely to use a thinking approach rather than a feeling approach in decision-making. However, many *collaborative* lawyers won't exhibit these attributes, tending to be more similar to the general public.

Collaborative mental health and financial professionals also share many common personality traits. A strong collaborative facilitator works from a set of core values consistent with the concepts of empowerment, commitment, collaboration, and learning.

Obviously, mental health professionals in general tend to be sensitive to others' feelings. They are more aware than most of how people are feeling and how to engage them. By focusing on body language, eye contact, and tone — they demonstrate good active listening.

Both mental health and financial facilitators tend to be better able to perceive and respond to group dynamics. They are tactful, especially in touchy situations when group discussions lose focus. They have a good sense of timing, knowing when to end a discussion or when to continue it. They are resourceful and creative, especially in situations where meetings don't proceed as expected.

Perhaps most importantly, the best facilitators understand that, although they are the leaders in many collaborative teams, they aren't the center of attention. They're relaxed and have a good sense of humor.

Effective financial professionals are good listeners who strive to make the parties comfortable in discussing their personal situations. Good communication skills are vital in the complicated and overwhelming financial issues to be resolved. They must be trustworthy and ethical. Their creative side enables them to think outside the box for solutions to the parties' unique circumstances. They should be optimistic and enthusiastic.

Understanding the different personality types is essential for the entire team, especially for facilitators, so that task assignments are given to the ones who will make the greatest contribution with the most effectiveness. To increase successful interaction with each other, team members should also understand their unique personalities, the other team members and their clients.

Avoid teaming up with those who primarily act from their reptilian brain, who focus on victory for their client and defeat for the opposing party. They may maximize monetary gain and status, while trying to make the other side look bad. And they'll want to control the process.

Less problematic, but still not ideal, are those who think ultra-socially. They focus on ensuring that the rules of society are respected and followed in a logical, civil, and orderly way. They desire that matters be settled in a dispassionate manner and with the goal of furthering a well-functioning and equitable society as a whole. Instead, seek out team members who think from their limbic brain, who will strive to uncover how the clients are feeling. They're reassuring and comforting, trying to reduce emotional pain and to keep relationships intact. They work to keep those around them healthy and happy.

In a society that emphasizes individual performance and

achievements, some people are uncomfortable working in the team dynamic. However, teams almost always outperform individuals, especially in settings like this, in which multiple skills, judgments, and experiences are needed. Each team member brings his own, particular strength to the team, whether it is the psychological and emotional understanding of the facilitator, the mathematical abilities of the financial professional, or the legal and advisory knowledge of the lawyers. And the team, as a whole, is worth more than the individual parts.

In traditional litigation, the attorney has to perform all these roles, whether skilled or not.

A team will work well when:

1. Its members have synergy, i.e. they know and like each other and are bound together by their commonalities;
2. Its members have unambiguous boundaries, limitations on each member's role, and they don't compete for attention;
3. It has shared vision and value, clear directions and unambiguous goals;
4. It has respected authority and unambiguous leadership;
5. Its members understand how to communicate with each other;
6. Its members are willing to address stress-inducing issues and don't avoid conflict; and
7. Its members know when to have fun.

So how do you know when a team is *not* working well? Learn to identify false team harmony which can lead to distrust, power struggles, and an uncomfortable environment. Ultimately, it may lead to collaborative failure. To avoid it, promote open and honest dialogue among team members. At the first full team meeting, encourage each team member and client to explain why they chose to proceed collaboratively. Keep in mind that an individual's true motivation may not be verbally expressed, but instead, may become clear through his actions. By being candid about one's true motivations early in the process, the potential for disconnection can be discussed before it occurs.

Even before discussing the parties' goals at the first meeting, the team should review their underlying motivations. That way, the team can develop a game plan for dealing with conflicting motivations. Demonstrate to the clients that the team has developed options for dealing with such misalignments, and ask the clients for their input on how to handle these differences.

The team may be able to ignore misalignments that don't affect the parties' goals or interests. These things may be discussed further with the clients and professionals offline, or among the team offline, or by all participants during a joint meeting, to develop coping strategies. Explore the clients' varying motivations and attempt to align them as much as possible. Continually assess whether the game plan for dealing with misalignments needs to be modified. Focused and harmonized goals and interests support a cohesive environment.

Because empathy drives prosocial behaviors, choose highly empathic team members. Empathy motivates people towards virtue and away from vice. These skills guide good social interaction because they involve understanding other people's emotional states. Without it, teams fail to accomplish goals.

Be sure that everyone on the team understands the main objective of the collaborative process and is working together towards that goal. This process works towards reaching a settlement that meets both parties' most important interests, in contrast to litigation, in which each attorney works to win his client's position and to destroy his opponent.

Demonstrate your trust for your team members. During teleconferences and debriefs, specifically praise the good work that each one has accomplished. By focusing on behaviors and practices that enhance their performance, you'll encourage more positive behaviors. Give constructive feedback in a non-aggressive manner, and accept the same feedback graciously. Remember that good teams hold one another mutually accountable.

Most effective teams have a leader, but that may not be appropriate in the collaborative setting. If a team member takes the leadership role, it should be a neutral, not an attorney. When one of the attorneys leads, it may appear that the other attorney is too passive. In some venues, the mental health professional is the neutral who takes the leadership role, runs the meetings, creates the agendas, and is skilled at helping the team work effectively. In other venues, it's the financial neutral who leads.

Effective teams must agree on their working approach. Most communities adopt general protocols for proceeding. While these can be modified to meet the needs of specific parties or issues, they're a good starting point and help everyone proceed on the same page.

Teams are less threatened by change than individuals, so they adapt and respond better. Their flexibility offers more room for growth and change; teams more quickly veer away from behaviors that aren't working than individuals do.

It's important to give potential collaborative professionals a chance, even if you have preconceived notions about how well they'll function in the collaborative model. If your only experience with the person has been from the opposing side of a courtroom, you may never have had the opportunity to witness her agreeable and compassionate side. Most professionals who've been practicing collaborative divorce for any period of time can share a tale of a hated rival "bulldog" litigator whom they never expected would be appropriate for the collaborative model, but who, when afforded the opportunity, became a stellar example.

On the other hand, once you've given another professional a chance, if they've failed to perform collaboratively, don't team up with them again. One bad team member can destroy the entire process.

Celebrate your team's success. When a final agreement is reached, hold a congratulatory signing meeting at which the professionals don't charge the clients for their time, but instead, celebrate the team's victory. Pop a bottle of champagne, or have cake. Award the clients with certificates of their successful collaboration, or gift them with a symbol of their achievement, perhaps a crystal lotus as I do, or something similar. Encourage everyone to attend the final uncontested hearing, and make sure to let the judge and the rest of the courtroom know just how proud the clients and the rest of the team are that they were able to put together a marital settlement agreement collaboratively.

I served on two separate grievance committees of The Florida Bar, a three-year stint each time. Even today, the most common complaint filed against an attorney is that he fails to return phone calls. Family lawyers are those most often grieved, and the next most common complaint is actually made by the opposing party, that the lawyer in question *too effectively* represented the grievant's former spouse. Of course, the complaint is never framed up in those precise words, but that's what it always amounts to. Incredibly, one of the end results of the collaborative divorce process is that each participant truly appreciates how effective the other's attorney is. And so it was in our case for the Andersons.

The CP Co-Counsel

We finally came to the end of our first, stress-filled full team meeting. Both clients had many emotional issues that repeatedly bubbled up during our brief two hours together. The Andersons had finally agreed, resolving all of the substantive temporary issues that had been scheduled for that meeting. I could almost hear the collective sigh of relief from the team.

But the wife, Jenna, was frowning. While we finished the few procedural details, scheduling the next two full team meetings, as well as the two professionals telephone conferences preceding each one, she was already packing her briefcase. When she stood, she turned to her attorney, Karen, taking her completely by surprise. "When are we going to resolve the issue of my temporary

131

support?" (Zing!)

Karen sputtered slightly. "Jenna, I . . . we . . . there's only so much you can accomplish in one meeting. We haven't pulled together all of the documents necessary to accomplish that yet. In fact, you can see that Barry brought all of those documents for the financial neutral today, and she's requested additional documentation from each of you. You just need to be patient."

"Okay. Fine." She was clearly unhappy. She stood, slung her briefcase over her shoulder, and then turned to her husband, Barry. "Have you given Christine the statements from your checking account?" Her tone was accusatory; she had already deduced that he had not.

He responded quickly. "I gave her the statements from all of our accounts."

"From your personal checking, that you've been depositing your paycheck in since you moved out?" (Zing again!)

He stepped back. "No, I haven't."

I knew that he had his own issues with protecting his post-petition information. (Jenna's attorney had filed her petition for dissolution of marriage before we had all agreed to handle the matter collaboratively.) In that way, he and Jenna were similar; she was hoarding her savings, and he was hoarding his information. He had told me that Jenna was a control freak, that he didn't want her controlling his life, his income, or his expenditures any longer.

I interceded. "Jenna, we'll make sure that Christine gets all the relevant information before our next meeting."

I think that she was aware of this, because Karen had prepped her, but she was frustrated and frightened. With no ongoing support from Barry since he'd moved out three months earlier, she only had the rental income. She'd always had access to all of his financial information and was annoyed that he was "hiding" that from her now. But she'd just planted a land mine; I was worried that my client, Barry, might step on it.

Karen added, "We can't accomplish everything in the first meeting."

The facilitator stepped in. "Jenna, you need to be patient. You're okay for now. You folks have accomplished so much in such a short space of time. Look, it's not even 5:00 p.m. Let the professionals do their jobs and we'll get it done."

The first full team meeting was over, and each attorney met with her client briefly to make sure that they were both okay and to answer their questions. When I spoke with Barry, I complimented him. "Barry, I have to say I'm glad you weren't thrown by Jenna's attack and that you allowed me to field it. I thought that Linda handled it well, too." I went on, reflectively, "Poor Karen. You have to know that Jenna was well aware what issues were on the agenda for today. Karen's got to be having a hard time keeping her reined in."

Barry smiled ruefully. "You can tell her I think she's doing a great job. From my experience, thirty years of marriage, I know how hard that can be."

Afterwards, during our professional debrief, Karen apologized for not controlling her client well enough. I was sure to tell her of Barry's praise and that she was doing a fine job... not something attorneys are used to hearing from the "opposing counsel." Only in collaborative!

Chapter Ten

Issues to Discuss
With Your Collaborative Attorney

Withdrawal

If you aren't able to reach a settlement using the collaborative process, your attorney must withdraw his representation of you, and you'll probably need to retain a litigator to represent you in court. The clients' pledge *not* to litigate is an intrinsic component of this dispute resolution process. It enables both people to speak freely without worrying that their words may be used against them in court, creating a "safe" environment for negotiation.

Because this commitment is a formal agreement rather than a verbal promise, it builds trust in the process, so each party can anticipate a good outcome. The pledge incentivizes participants to focus on reaching a settlement rather than to fire their attorneys and litigate. That's a plus in a judicial system in which reaching a compromised settlement is nearly always a better alternative than throwing the dice by appealing to some judge, who doesn't know you or your kids, or share your values, for a decision.

Finally, the collaborative process eliminates the lawyer's ability to "stir the pot," whether by design or by accident. It also reduces the impact of the conflict of interest that every lawyer has with every client: in very simple terms, that conflict of interest stems from the fact that the attorney wants to make *more* money and the client wants to pay *less* money. The lawyer's sole job in the collaborative model is to help the clients satisfy their interests and settle their divorce issues without falling back on the traditional courtroom model of resolving their dissolution of marriage disputes. Thus, he has nothing to gain if he even inadvertently causes friction between the clients because, if they go to court, he gets fired!

Costs

You may pay substantial additional costs if you decide to litigate, because it's almost always costly. Few clients appreciate this until they've been involved in litigation and paid the invoices. The initial retainer is only the beginning, and it's never the largest slice of the "cost of legal services" pie. Once the litigation gets underway, the invoices just get larger and larger.

Why is this true? Rather than trying to settle matters amicably, trial attorneys tend to file motions for even the simplest of issues. This "motions practice" process leads to discovery games in which one party refuses to provide financial documents and the other party is forced to chase them down. This adds months and money to the process.

In the collaborative process, on the other hand, the transparency required enables both clients to simply ask each other for information; the other side provides it within days. And the confidentiality guarantee ensures that all of the information exchanged is still protected from prying public eyes.

In litigation, if one side hires an expert, then the other side had better do the same or risk losing the issue without putting up a fight. Thus ensues the battle of the experts where information is concealed and experts not only present material but must defend it from attack from the other side. This is why the cost of both sides' experts at trial is usually four times the cost of the neutral expert in the collaborative case.

Lawyers who litigate often engage in unnecessary discovery to avoid later accusations of legal malpractice. So trial attorneys take depositions which are needless in a collaborative approach. And, of course, both lawyers must appear at the depositions, as well as a court reporter to transcribe the proceedings, who is also paid for her time.

These are but three of the reasons that litigation tends to be expensive and hostile, and may destroy families who are already emotional and at odds with one another. The process fails to consider that, after the divorce, the parents must still deal with one another if children are involved. If you spend thousands of dollars trying to collaborate, give up, and opt to litigate, you'll likely have to start over, unable to take your collaborative material into the courtroom.

Cooperation

Is your spouse likely to cooperate with you in the collaborative process? Are either of you looking for retribution or punishment? Will he able consider other points of view, or is he only focused on what she wants? Even if he is, and even if he's angry, is he susceptible to reason, when push comes to shove? Will he put the best interests of your children ahead of his own? Does he understand the value of maintaining as good a relationship with you as possible? Will your spouse be able to act maturely and respectfully toward you? Is he seeking revenge or does he wish to resolve your divorce as amicably as possible?

Retribution and punishment won't happen during the collaborative process, and those who want such outcomes will most certainly prefer to litigate.

Transparency

Are you willing to disclose all financial information and information regarding your children to your spouse? Are you concerned that your spouse won't make full disclosure to you? How can we encourage him to be entirely transparent? Candidly sharing information on each side is important to a good collaborative outcome.

In addition, trusting that the other spouse is reciprocating is important as well. If you aren't confident that your spouse can act transparently, what would encourage him to do so? Three key considerations may help: money, time, and personal control of the outcome. Perhaps the idea that litigation will cost more money and that, if forced to litigate, he may be forced to pay your litigator's fees as well? Or maybe the idea that it will likely take longer than collaborative? Or the idea that, in the collaborative process, clients can tailor-make their agreements to reflect their personal values, rather than a judge ordering them only as the law allows?

Interests

Not positions. Do you have realistic expectations for the outcome? Are you able to be flexible in your demands and explore your interests rather than your positions? Are you willing to negotiate a settlement based on interests rather than positional negotiation?

If you insist on a specific outcome, you're taking a position, rather than negotiating an interest. If your spouse takes the opposing position, then you'll only achieve deadlock. However, if you discuss each side's underlying interests, you're more likely to uncover different possible outcomes.

Most collaborative cases begin with the clients identifying their interests and goals, and during each meeting thereafter, the professionals will remind them of these. Positional bargaining versus interest-based negotiation is a fundamental shift in thinking that lets go of labels in favor of the bigger picture. Once interests are identified, then the team will brainstorm options to meet them, rather than clinging to a single option that only satisfies one position.

A classic demonstration of the difference between a position and an interest is illustrated by the following scenario. Imagine that you and your spouse have one orange to share between you, and you both want the entire orange. You both *need* one orange. But there is only one.

If you focus on your positions alone, i.e. that you each want the orange, one of you will win it and one of you will lose it. Or you may cut it in half, and neither of you will be satisfied. However, if you focus on your separate interests in the orange, you may be able to find a win-win solution. Perhaps you want the zest so that you can make a dessert. Your spouse may want the pulp to make juice. Understanding your interests will allow you to win the peel, and your spouse to win the pulp—a win-win solution for you both.

Most collaborative divorces begin with the spouses identifying their goals, and, during each meeting thereafter, the professionals keep those goals in front of them. The team works to uncover the underlying interests behind any positions the clients may take, and tries to identify and discuss resolutions that satisfy that interest. Enlarging the range of alternatives by linking potential solutions to underlying issues helps satisfy the needs of both people to the greatest extent possible.

Power Imbalance

Are you comfortable sitting in the same room with your spouse and being transparent, or are you concerned that there's an imbalance of power?

When domestic violence, mental health issues, and/or substance abuse issues are involved, divorce can be much more difficult. However, these issues don't mean that collaborative practice isn't appropriate for you. In fact, it may be even more apropos for you.

Vulnerable clients generally fare poorly in the hostile environment of traditional courtroom divorce. A collaborative team supports both spouses, and includes a neutral mental health professional or an aligned mental health coach. The case may be more challenging, but this process is likely the best option for individuals with these or similar issues.

Trust

Are you concerned that your spouse has ulterior motives for seeking a divorce or for resisting a divorce? Will your distrust affect your ability to openly collaborate?

Trust is a crucial component; it requires each party to believe that the other is being transparent. If you think that your spouse has ulterior motives, you probably won't trust him. In this model, the facilitator and/or coach may be able to work through your concerns in order to gain the trust that will help you during the collaborative process and that will last long afterwards.

"Mental Health"

Are you or your spouse opposed to having a mental health professional on the team? These collaborative professionals act as the facilitators, the communications coordinators, and the team leaders. They aren't there to offer therapy and their presence does not imply that one or both clients are mentally ill. Instead they concentrate on eliminating the stressful communication and emotional issues that can hinder negotiation. Sometimes they open communication by translating what one team member may be trying to say for the others. They also grease the problem solving wheels. Finally, they keep the team on task to effect a timely resolution.

Voluntary

Do you understand that the collaborative process is voluntary? Either party may withdraw for any reason at any time.

In sum, let's review:

1. **Withdrawal** – Are you comfortable with your promise not to litigate and understand you must find a trial lawyer if the process terminates?

2. **Costs** – Do you appreciate how costs are apportioned differently in litigation and in the collaborative process?

3. **Cooperation** – Can you and your spouse cooperate with the best interests of your children and/or your family in mind and put aside any vengeful thinking?

4. **Transparency** – Are you willing to disclose all of your information and put aside any thoughts of sandbagging your spouse?

5. **Interests** – Do you understand why it is important to focus on your interests and not on any positions you might already have taken?

6. **Power Imbalance** – Are you comfortable that the team can ensure that there is no power imbalance between you and your spouse?

7. **Trust** – Are you willing to trust your spouse and the team?

8. **Mental Health** – Are you comfortable with the role of the mental health professional on your team?

9. **Voluntary** – Do you accept that this process is completely voluntary, for both of you, and that either of you can opt out at any time?

These are all important issues to understand and discuss with your attorney. It's crucial that you both are on the same page when you enter into the collaborative relationship in order to avoid disappointment with either your lawyer or the process, so that he can effectively represent your interests.

Chapter Eleven

Interest-Based Negotiations[3]

It may feel unnatural to negotiate your interests, rather than your positions, especially during a stressful period in your life, when you want to put up walls. But position-based negotiation is adversarial, only considering the needs of one side, and limiting good alternatives that might be satisfying, so it stymies the negotiation process.

In contrast, focusing on interests rather than on positions enables people to negotiate reasonably without threats, intimidation, or ultimatums. It avoids a deadlock and allows discussion of each person's underlying interests, which leads to uncovering different outcomes. Brainstorming multiple options for goals can lead to satisfaction for both parties.

Identify Your Interests

Thus, in collaboration, the first step is to develop your interests. Identifying goals allows for more bargaining room and helps spouses discover more than one way to resolve each issue. It's also important for you both to prioritize so that the team can work towards achieving your most important goals and allowing you to compromise on your less important ones.

---

[3] The incisive work on this subject is *Getting to Yes (Negotiating Agreement Without Giving In)*, by Roger Fisher and William Ury. Although originally published well over 30 years ago, this practical primer on the fundamentals of negotiation remains the leading work in the field of conflict resolution today.

Later, you will pay attention to your spouse's interests, as well, as they are also key to creating a successful settlement offer.

Gathering Your Information

The second step is gathering information from both people. Unlike adversarial discovery in litigation, transparency and confidentiality reduces stressful concern that information will become public. The neutral facilitator or, in the two-coach model, the two coaches will meet individually with both of you to discuss your goals, your issues, your concerns, and your relationship history. She will then prepare a report of your interviews and her perceptions and provide it to the entire professional team so that everyone has a better understanding of both of you, your personalities, your strengths, and your weaknesses. She will advise them on how to avoid pitfalls in the process based on your individual personality traits and histories.

The neutral financial professional will also work with you both to compile your financial documents. By reviewing the documents provided, he should be able to determine whether an important document was concealed. If it's determined that one party isn't being transparent, the team will encourage that client to be more open. It may be necessary for the team to address some temporary issue in order to facilitate this.

If not, the collaborative process must be terminated.

Discuss the Law

The third step is to discuss how one might apply the law to the facts. Lawyers have very different and often quite adamant views on what role the law should play in the collaborative process. Some believe that it should have absolutely no role and that it should not even be discussed. They feel that to do so would undermine the goal of collaborative practice, that is to say to help clients reach the best settlement agreement possible for them and for their unique families, regardless of what the law says.

Other attorneys ardently believe that our job is to educate our clients about the law so that they may make informed and educated decisions. They consider it legal malpractice not to tell the client what might happen if their case went in front of the judge.

It's possible that one or both of you have previously discussed "the law" with other lawyers, as well as with your friends and family. You may therefore have misconceptions as to what the law is, and/or how it may be applied to your situation. Once both clients have signed the collaborative participation agreement, it will be important for your collaborative professionals to uncover and correct any erroneous beliefs. If not, they're likely to affect how fairly and reasonably you or your spouse are able to negotiate, infecting the process.

On the other hand, it may be helpful to use the law to strengthen any settlement agreement you may have reached, safeguarding both your agreement and you, the clients, against future legal challenges.

Further, you look to your lawyer for guidance. Don't be surprised if he reminds you that, regardless of what "the law" might say, it's always applied by a person, a judge who doesn't know you or your kids, or share your values, and who might be having a bad day, the day he makes the decision. Or it may take him so long to get back to considering your case that he's forgotten some of the details "proved up" in trial.

Except in extreme circumstances or with respect to certain legal issues regarding the rights of minor children, you should both work towards an agreement that is in your families' best interests, regardless of what you might believe the law requires.

Brainstorm Your Options

The fourth step is to problem solve, to generate options. By defining each client's goals first, your team can then generate multiple settlement options to accomplish those. Brainstorming provides a free and open environment in which everyone on the team participates. The team actively listens when brainstorming, but the process should have a relaxed and casual feel.

Everyone will be encouraged to think outside the box and discouraged from criticizing any ideas at this stage. Additionally, you'll notice that the team avoids rewarding ideas because people may focus on those suggestions and close their minds to possible alternatives. Judgment and analysis at this point will stunt idea generation and limit creativity. By exploring as many alternatives as possible, you'll enjoy the best chance of reaching a settlement that addresses your most important interests.

Negotiate Agreement

The fifth step is reaching an agreement. Once you have brainstormed as many ideas as the team thinks possible, you'll tweak and trade options until a final settlement has been reached. Evaluate ideas *after* you conclude your brainstorming session; this is the time to explore solutions further, using conventional approaches. Determine how your interests can be met by the many possible solutions. Discuss the cost and benefit to each of you for each proposal.

The team may ask each of you to step into the other's shoes and analyze whether you would be happy with the proposal if you were your spouse. Brainstorming enables participants are able to explore many scenarios in pursuit of an effective settlement agreement.

Draft Your Agreement

The final step is to formalize the agreement. One or both of the attorneys will draft the agreement for the rest of the professionals to review. Once they've approved it, the attorneys will each discuss it with their clients. Additional negotiations may take place at this stage, as you or your spouse remember details forgotten during the team meetings, or identify issues suggested by the written draft agreement.

Celebrate Your Success

Once both of you approve the agreement, you'll sign it. Many collaborative teams hold a celebratory signing meeting at no charge for their clients. Many teams will bring champagne, cake, or some other festive treat. They'll praise the clients and the team for working together to come to the agreement.

Once the agreement is signed, in many jurisdictions, one or both of you attends a five-minute hearing at which your attorney "proves up" the agreement. The judge will enter a final judgment ratifying the terms of your agreement and granting your divorce.

This is a success story about moving parties from staking out and defending their positions to figuring out how to get their true interests met.

The Position

I was late to the monthly meeting of my local collaborative practice POD[4] where we confer over a glass of wine or a bottle of beer about, among other things, how best to resolve novel issues that may have arisen in our cases. I was feeling a bit rushed, *and* the traffic was bad. Driving in rush-hour makes me worry that I'll miss it when the car ahead of me stops suddenly, and I'll smack right into it. So my heart jumped into my throat at the odd "brrring" of my cell phone.

Brad Godot, one of my newer collaborative divorce clients, wanted to discuss an e-mail I'd forwarded to him a few days before, from Elena, who represented his wife. She'd asked us to consider her client's "request" that Brad agree to list their Bayview house, one of the clients' several rental properties, for sale. She explained. "Tracie said that she and Brad had started the process to put the Bayview house on the market for sale before he moved out." Tracie had found a realtor, Christine Brighton, who planned to list it for $15,000 over the amount for which she believed it could sell.

This e-mail surprised me. Earlier that week, we'd had our first

---

4 Professional and Organizational Development group.

full team meeting. There, we'd successfully resolved initial and urgent financial issues such as payment of the neutral professionals' retainer fees and the wife's need for temporary support. We'd also addressed a couple of unusual issues, the son's college tuition payment, and due in two weeks, and the annual $30,000 life insurance premium that was due in just ten days.

Tracie hadn't raised the issue of the rental property, despite having met with the facilitator to discuss the agenda beforehand.

It wasn't that Brad wasn't amenable, as far as I could tell, on multiple issues. As an attorney he'd come to me for a collaborative divorce because he knew better than to go to court. Most lawyers do. They come to me to explore the range of courtless divorce options, and which one will best suit their families and their circumstances, as well as their pocketbooks.

We'd yet to hold our second full team meeting, in which longer-term financial issues could be addressed. In the meantime, the clients were busy collecting documents and information for the financial neutral to review and collate before making her recommendations. In fact, we'd had to postpone our second meeting once already because Tracie was dragging her feet, getting information to Karlyn at a snail's pace, which we all understood; she didn't want the divorce.

Brad had told me, at our initial consultation, that he'd been accumulating residential properties for years, in his efforts to create a second income to supplement his law practice. But now, while I drove to my POD meeting, he was telling me that he didn't want to fight over the properties. "Brad, is it true that you two agreed to sell the property?"

He quickly said, "Well, I think that's an exaggeration. She suggested it because there wasn't a tenant at the time. But we didn't really have a discussion. It's not a hard property to rent out and it's not really a good time to sell, but I didn't want to argue."

So if he agreed to sell, it wouldn't be because he wanted to. "Would you lose money if you sold it for the price she's talking about?"

"No, I don't think so, but it would be close. We'd probably about break even."

"Correct me if I'm wrong, but isn't that the property you

moved into when you moved out of the marital home?"

"Well, yes, but you know . . . ."

"You're not spending all of your nights there, am I right?"

"No, and I know Tracie really wants to know where I *am* spending my time. She texted me the other morning at 1 a.m. and asked me where I was. She said she was standing outside the house and knew I wasn't there. But I don't think that's any of her business."

"Well, you and I talked about that already, and I haven't changed my opinion." I commented, equably. "At this point, I don't think it's relevant to the issues between you, but if it becomes relevant, we will have to disclose it."

"I know. I just don't want to start another fight for no good reason."

"So, what's Tracie's real interest in trying to push the sale forward when you two hadn't *really* made that decision as of when you moved out?"

I could hear him breathing over the purring sound of my car's engine. He began tentatively, "Obviously she wants to address the issue of where I'm living and this is her way of doing it. If we sell the house, then she thinks I'll have to reveal that I'm not really living there full-time."

"Brad, I don't want to cause a problem here if there isn't one." I chose my words carefully. "But I think what's interesting is that, as far as we know, Elena hasn't asked Tracie what her interest in selling the house so quickly is. She's simply re-stating her position, that you two had agreed to sell the house, and that she wants it done as soon as possible. We can agree to that, of course. But weren't you considering making an offer to keep all of the rental properties, so that Tracie could retain both the marital home and all of the marital cash in exchange?"

"Absolutely. It makes good sense for me to keep the rentals. I'm better equipped to deal with them. I work in a firm where I have an associate who deals exclusively with foreclosures. And I have another associate who deals primarily with landlord-tenant problems. Never mind that I'm a real estate lawyer myself. It makes more sense for me to keep them and for Tracie to get the marital home and the cash.

"I'll be supporting her until I die regardless." He made this statement with equanimity. He wasn't angry; he'd made his peace with it, even before he came to see me. It was the price of his divorce, and she deserved that after 30 years of marriage, staying home to raise their son, and making it comfortable for him.

As I considered how to respond to Elena's inquiry, I was luckily, nearly at my POD meeting and Karlyn would also be attending. One of our goals is to explore real-life collaborative problems we're facing and obtain outside, objective input from the others on solving them. So I decided to raise the issue.

Once I had summarized the situation, I asked Karlyn, "You know the personalities involved here. I think I should point out to Elena that 1) my client tells me that there was no such agreement in place, and 2) she should ask her client what her goal is in selling this property so quickly. I should remind her that this is the property that my client happens to be living in right now, and, given his 'position' that they never agreed to sell it, we should probably have a clear and transparent discussion regarding the clients' interests in this property before they make a decision. What do you think?"

Karlyn is very experienced in collaborative negotiations. I respect her opinion. She reflected before responding. "Elena hasn't had that many cases yet. I think she'll appreciate a soft-handed approach if you simply remind her of the need to address the real interests involved, as opposed to simply pursuing what her client has stated as her position. I think it's very possible that she hasn't focused on the fact that Tracie's pushing a position, instead of an interest. "

"Great! That makes me feel much better."

I carefully worded my response, and ran it by Karlyn for her approval prior to sending the following:

> Elena, thanks for bringing this issue to my attention. My client tells me that he and Tracie had only "started" talking about whether to put the house on the market. He's not convinced that he wants to do that and, given that he may get that house in the equitable distribution of the clients' assets, it doesn't

make sense to do anything precipitous. That said, please understand that he's *not* saying "no."

More importantly, it seems to me that your client has taken a position here without exploring what her goal is. Why does Tracie want "to move forward with selling the house as soon as possible?" What is her interest in unloading it quickly? It might make sense for her to discuss this with Anna before our next full team meeting? What do you think?

I was surprised when Elena replied:

Thanks for your response, but it raises some questions for me. When we were just starting this process, I asked about Bayview while alerting you that Tracie was under the impression that Brad was not really living there. You replied that Brad and Tracie "had agreed that the Bayview House can be put on the market or rented and, in that event, he would move out." Maybe Brad has changed his mind? Do you know why? Could he perhaps have simply forgotten about his agreement with Tracie?

I think Tracie's reasoning in seeking the sale of the Bayview house may be multi-faceted, but I know she is concerned about the wastefulness of it standing empty, and I believe she is finding her role in the family's properties overwhelming (although that is coming from my observations rather than a discussion with her.)

As I had simply been a conduit in the earlier discussion, I *had* forgotten it. Brad and I met in my office to discuss it.

"Elena didn't answer my question about interests, but asked other questions instead. We don't *have* to answer them but we should be forewarned. I *do* believe that 'yes, Brad *did* change mind' is a right answer, if true. If you like, I'll tell her that we reassessed and the offer you ultimately intend to make negates the reasonableness of 'unloading' the property."

Brad crossed his legs and leaned forward, agreeing. "Tracie and I had that talk before beginning this process and getting a handle on how it works. She suggested selling the home and I didn't object. But now it seems like the team can help us handle the property distribution in a more organized fashion."

I let Elena know this much in a quick e-mail, but Brad and I agreed that I should address the issue Elena had raised, that Tracie was possibly being overwhelmed by her responsibility for the rentals, with the other team members.

During our professionals' teleconference the following day, we *did* discuss that Tracie might be out of her depth managing several rentals, "especially because she's really being affected by this divorce," according to Elena. I pointed out that Brad had left them in her care so that she would feel more in control, a need of hers of which he was very much aware, and which Anna, our facilitator, had also brought to everyone's attention. We resolved to address Tracie's interest at the next full team meeting.

Shortly after this call, Anna notified the other professionals that Tracie had contacted her, frustrated because she felt that she was not getting direct answers on many issues, including the Bayview sale. Anna and she then discussed *why* she had focused on unloading the Bayview property. Anna reported that Tracie wasn't emotionally or financially in a position to manage all of the rentals at the same time as she was trying to figure out how to live the rest of her life without Brad.

At the following full team meeting, we were finally able to make some forward movement. Instead of agreeing to sell Bayview, Brad suggested that he take over getting the repairs needed there accomplished, whether the couple sold the property or not, retaining the contractors, overseeing the work, and paying the bills.

Tracie was relieved that, as she saw it, "progress was finally being made," although, at the team debrief after, Elena shared that she was just happy to have Bayview off her plate. Brad was happy that he had protected the possibility that he might retain all of the rentals in the eventual divorce agreement. That momentum helped the clients to move forward on resolving other issues.

Gently pointing out to Elena that Tracie was being inappropriately positional allowed the team, first, to identify the true interests underlying her position, and, second, to therefore guide the clients onward in the process, a collaborative success.

Chapter Twelve

Communication

One of the most important tools of a collaborative professional is the ability to communicate well and to understand the communication of others.[5] As much as fifty-five percent of communication is non-verbal: facial expression, posture, gestures, behaviors, and inferences. Thirty-eight percent is tone and inflection. Only seven percent is an individual's actual choice of words!

There are often conflicts between spoken words and tone or body language. When this happens, the tone and body language control. For example, if a person rolls her eyes while saying "thank you," she isn't *really* appreciative, even though her words say otherwise.

Communication varies by culture. So if you are working with team members from diverse cultures, it may be necessary to learn how to interpret their communications and how better to communicate with them. You don't want to inadvertently insult a team member, or to feel insulted, merely because your communication patterns differ.

Inability to communicate effectively frustrates people.

---

[5] When I was a very young lawyer, in practice for just six years, Deborah Tannen published *That's Not What I Meant!*, her seminal work on how conversational style makes or breaks relationships. I still have my original copy, as well as her later work, *You Just Don't Understand*, now a classic in the field of interpersonal relations. Any serious collaborative practitioner will have read both of these.

Consider an infant just learning to speak. When you don't understand him, he is likely to become exasperated, to throw a tantrum, and even to cry.

An adult with poor communication skills suffers from similar frustrations. To help this person express his true feelings, one must listen actively, ask questions, and repeat how one understands him to feel to correctly comprehend his comments. Sometimes reframing what he has said, in words other than the ones he has chosen, allows him, as well as the others on the team, to hear himself better.

Prior to the first full team meeting, the facilitator usually meets with each client to discuss her goals, issues, concerns, and relationship history. He will also discuss the protocols of conduct, and will explain how she can help to make the process as effective and successful as possible. This will include arming her with techniques to stay calm, one of her most important tasks during the process, as well as with methods to enhance her ability to communicate with her spouse, such as active listening skills.

He prepares a comprehensive report to help the team understand both clients, including tips on how to communicate without causing them to become defensive or to shut down.

Common triggers for divorcing spouses are finances, trust, loyalty, or parenting. While a client's trigger may seem irrational to the team because the client is in a very emotional place, it must be adequately addressed or it will impair the team's ability to proceed effectively. Team members should recognize these triggers so that they may choose their words carefully and re-frame negative comments.

Before meetings, a lawyer will often remind her client that, to work towards settlement efficiently, it's important to communicate appropriately during the meeting. She'll remind him to be cognizant of body language, facial expressions, word choices, and tone. She'll suggest avoiding "you statements," which make other people defensive. People who feel attacked often react by defending themselves, counterattacking, or withdrawing. These responses hinder the collaborative process, so well considered communication is important.

It is easier to identify what participants should *not* do, rather than tell them what they *should* do. The following types of communication should be avoided during the collaborative process:

✓ Focusing on unnecessary discussions of the past and assessing blame instead of focusing on the future and resolving conflict;

✓ Failing to express your true interests;

✓ Forgetting to keep shared goals and true interests in mind;

✓ Distracting the team from the true issues;

✓ Failing to be honest and transparent;

✓ Taking a competitive, impatient, ordering, commanding stance or interrogating;

✓ Using "you" sentences instead of "I" sentences;

✓ Advising and lecturing other team members about what is "best" and assuming that you have all the answers;

✓ Conversely, acting too passively in order to keep the peace; or

✓ Withdrawing or otherwise avoiding conflict altogether;

✓ Neglecting to ask for a break or to adjourn when a participant feels that progress has ceased or he is about to lose control;

✓ Attempting to solve everyone else's problems;

✓ Being impatient;

✓ Using sarcasm and being discourteous; and

✓ Preaching.

Instead, remind clients to focus on compromise and collaboration. Each side will need to give up certain things to resolve the matter. Together, both clients will work towards a win/win solution that meets each party's most important interests.

COLLABORATION SUCCESS INDICATORS

SUCCESSFUL PEOPLE

UNSUCCESSFUL PEOPLE

Put the children first

Fail to put children first and even put them in the middle

SUCCESSFUL PEOPLE

COMMUNICATION

- Able to identify partner's needs and wishes and empathize
- Able to trust the other party
- Willing to be transparent
- Express their own thoughts and feelings clearly and succinctly
- Speak in normal tones throughout a meeting, while foregoing intimidation and ignoring the intimidation of others
- Forego interrupting the other participants

PERFORMANCE

- Willing to search for solutions that help both of them
- Able to confer with the other participant in the same room and discuss matters with the other participant
- Receptive to suggestions and alternatives and cooperative
- Remain in a meeting regardless of what is said
- Arrive prepared
- Appreciate realistic expectations for what will be accomplished

UNSUCCESSFUL PEOPLE

COMMUNICATION

- Accuse, blame, complain, and use "you" statements
- Make long-winded explanations and abuse e-mail and the telephone
- Speak for the other client, rather than speaking for themselves
- Withhold pertinent information
- Can't engage in necessary and difficult conversations
- Bring invisible shadow advisors into collaborative meetings
- Badger the other client
- Fail to listen actively

PERFORMANCE

- Lock into a position or attach to one particular outcome
- Argue over personal property of minimal value
- Fail to follow through on agreements
- Reschedule or arrive late to meetings
- Arrive at meetings under the influence or actively abusing substances
- Fail to take care of their personal health, both physically and mentally
- Unrealistic about budget and cash flow or misunderstand financials

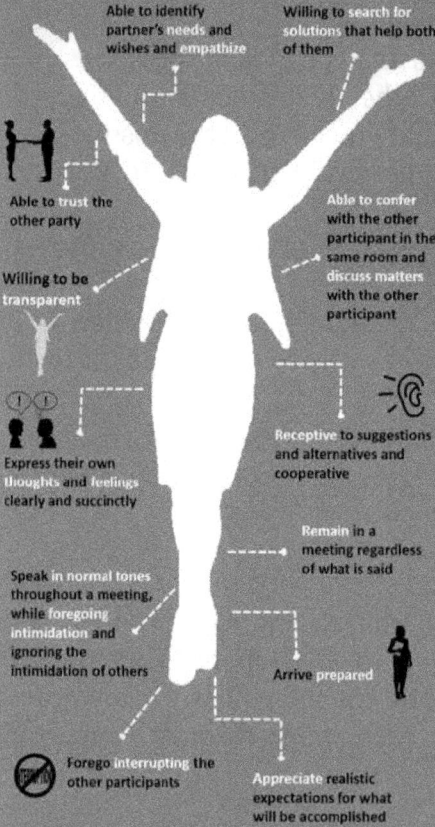

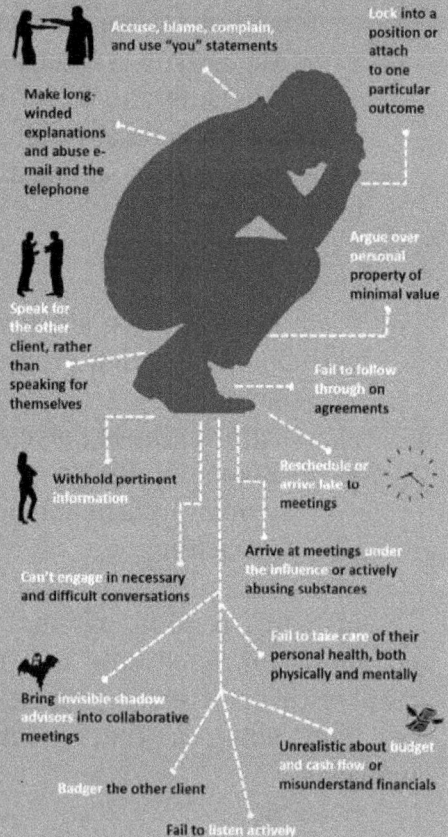

Copyright © 2015 OpenPalmLaw

158

We tell our clients to update the beneficiaries on their retirement accounts and life insurance policies after their divorces have been finalized. We recommend that they close all joint checking and savings accounts as soon as possible, when checks and any on-line payments have cleared the bank. And that they open new accounts individually, preferably in different banks so that no one at the bank is likely to make an error, not realizing the change in the relationship between the two former spouses. We recommend that they create new estate plans, including new wills, new trusts, new health-care surrogates, new living wills, and new powers of attorney as soon as they are single again.

Nevertheless, it's amazing what people neglect to do when they have other things on their minds. Is this because we failed to communicate well enough, or is it because the stress of litigation makes it impossible for them to hear?

The Beneficiary

I represented a twenty-five-year-old woman named Dawn Snow who became pregnant while dating her boyfriend. Although they were living together, they broke up before she had the baby. She came to me to discuss obtaining child support from him.

Although this was in 2001, she was dressed straight out of the sixties, with the clicking beads, the tie-died ankle-length skirt, and a matching sash tied around her head, her long dark hair falling well past her waist. Her mother accompanied her to our consultation, as did her month-old son. She nursed him during our initial meeting, without so much as a "by-your-leave." Although I'm a heterosexual woman, it was still distracting. I had to force myself to focus on her face while she angrily described how she had walked out on her boyfriend during an argument, "and I never went back!"

When I approached her ex, he was quite willing to be involved in the infant's life, and to pay child support. In fact, he had been trying to get information about their son since they'd broken up, but Dawn would have none of it. No matter how I counseled her, she was so angry with him, and so heedless of her child's best interests, that she wanted no part of him, other than his money.

Although she was the one who had terminated their relationship, he'd moved on. She hadn't and was intent on getting revenge. She was absolutely disinterested in resolving the matter collaboratively, although I had spoken with him about the possibility before we filed suit and he was amenable.

We quickly got the matter heard in court. At first, we tried to mediate, but Dawn was unwilling to concede any timesharing with "my son." (I attempted to coach her to refer to the baby as "our son," so that her possessiveness wouldn't be so blatant, but that was a fiasco.) She expounded at interminable length how she had to breast feed the child every hour or so, and how it just wasn't the same if she pumped. She only wanted him to visit their son in her apartment while she supervised. "He has no clue how to handle a baby," she contended.

I tried to explain that every parent is a parent for the first time, as she was herself, but she wasn't interested. Even her mother failed to talk some sense into her. Her only interest was in denying the young man any right to parent their child.

Eventually, she was awarded the child support, but the court also gave him the right to visit with the child fairly frequently. (This was back when visitation and custody were still the terms that we used, and dads were lucky to get 40% of the overnights with their children. But he did.)

In an obvious attempt to obstruct his visitation, Dawn moved from Tampa to Orlando. (This was also before one had to request permission from the court to relocate the child more than 50 miles away.) Nevertheless, he visited with his son every other weekend, Friday through Monday morning, trekking over to Orlando to retrieve him on Fridays and driving him back to my client's apartment on Monday mornings.

Halfway through the case her mother stopped paying her bills. (Dawn had never paid them.) I don't know why; perhaps she was just fed up with her daughter's hostility. But I felt an allegiance to the child and, because the end of the litigation was near, I continued to work while the soap opera played out. It took longer than I had anticipated, and my client ended up owing me about $6000. It could have been worse.

Her mother, who'd co-signed the agreement retaining my services, filed her petition for Chapter 7 bankruptcy protection shortly after the court entered its final judgment of paternity, visitation, and support. So she was no longer obligated to pay my bills. However, the young woman herself never sought bankruptcy protection. Instead, she went on welfare.

I concluded that I'd never be paid and put the matter out of my mind. My grandmother had always said, "There's no use crying over spilt milk."

Several years later, I received a phone call from a woman whose name sounded familiar. She introduced herself, "I'm Miriam Pearson. I'm James Pearson's mother."

"I'm sorry. I'm not making the connection. How do I know you?"

She quickly explained with a tremble in her voice. "You represented Dawn Snow years ago. My son Jimmy was the father of her child."

"Oh, yes. Of course. I remember him now." I paused, absorbing the implications. "Was?"

She sighed heavily, the tears quivering on the edge of her voice. "He died last week in a hit-and-run accident."

"I'm so sorry." And I was. He had seemed a lovely, responsible young man. So unlike my client. I waited a beat. "How can I help?"

She took a breath, settling. "Well, actually, the question is how I can help you."

I waited for her to clarify. It didn't take long. "I know that Dawn still owes you money. Jimmy married, but he never changed the beneficiary on his first life insurance policy, so the insurance company is about to write a check to Dawn." He'd been so responsible that he'd bought life insurance and had named his live-in girlfriend as the beneficiary when he was just twenty-five! "He told me how nice you were to him, and how you tried to reason with Dawn about his visitation and all that. I think that, if Jimmy's wife isn't going to benefit, at least you should get paid."

I cannot convey my amazement that she should feel this way, that she should want to honor my attempts to "collaborate" in the face of Dawn's aggressive antagonism. How unusual to be so appreciated by the "opposing party" in a litigated matter.

It wasn't difficult for me to ensure that the life insurance (a small policy, but it did cover my fees) was paid to my firm, instead of to my deadbeat client, although she fought me tooth-and-nail. It did require a trip to the courthouse, but I go there fairly often anyway, so it's not like it was out of my way.

In the following story, one sees how effective communication delivered in the right fashion can be.

The Lesson

Mia never really enjoyed her adolescence. By 16, she had given birth to Chelsea, whose teenaged father was quick to shirk his parental duties. Mia and Chelsea lived with Mia's mother until Mia was able to finish high school, but, in the meantime, she bounced from man to man, subconsciously trying to find someone mature enough to help her manage her very adult responsibilities.

When she met James at the local car wash, he was manning the register. He was three years her senior, and immediately took to Chelsea. Before Mia knew it, the two of them had moved in with him.

But he had bigger aspirations than clerking at the car wash. After they'd lived together for several months, he suggested that they both enroll in junior college to become occupational therapy assistants (OTAs). Mia agreed and they eventually obtained their degrees.

When she became pregnant again at 19, it was a blessing, rather than a curse. He proposed, and she was thrilled to truly create her own family. She thought that they'd be together forever. They were both excited to welcome their son, Sean, into the world.

As time passed, they struggled with the problems that many young families face. But as they matured, they grew apart. Because

James made more money than anyone else in his family, and felt it his duty to support his mother and younger brother, they also struggled financially, which added another layer of stress.

Over the course of their eleven-year marriage, both of them behaved in ways that negatively impacted their trust and respect for each other. They had disparate personality types. Initially, their differences had attracted them to one another; they felt that they complemented each other, which they certainly did as far as their parenting styles were concerned. (After all, that's why kids need two parents, to demonstrate both sides of the coin.) Unfortunately, these differences ultimately drove them apart.

A few years into their marriage, Mia spoke with her pastor about their problems. She asked James to attend couples counseling, but he refused. He knew they needed help, but hadn't grown up in an environment in which counseling was acceptable.

Eventually, she moved out, taking the kids with her. He often visited both children, and gave Mia money for bills, but only when she asked for it. And she hated to ask.

When she lost her job, her finances grew strained beyond her ability to manage. Although he had a stable, well-paying job, the market for OTAs in Tampa was limited and Mia had difficulty finding a decent position.

He'd recently moved from their old one-bedroom apartment into a three-bedroom house so that his mother, his brother, and his aunt could live with him. Mia understood that none of them contributed to the rent, so he was taking care of all of them, but he wasn't taking care of his own children! After years of living hand-to-mouth, and with no assurance of how much support she could rely on from James, or when he'd pay it, she'd finally had enough. At the end of an angry diatribe, she told him that she wanted a divorce, but what she really wanted was a reliable amount of financial aid, i.e. child support.

This upset him; after all, he contributed his share whenever she asked him for help. What he didn't understand was that she didn't readily admit that she *needed* help, and it was hard for her to come right out and ask him for money.

Pissed off, he petitioned for divorce.

One evening after getting home from work, Mia was making

dinner for the kids when the doorbell rang. Curious, she answered the door. A young man she didn't know handed her a sheaf of papers and stated, mechanically, "You've been served. You have 20 days to file your answer." Then he walked away.

She was startled . . . and frightened. What was this? She glanced at the caption of the top page. It said "James Richard Nation versus Mia Leslie Nation," in bold capped letters on the left hand side. In the middle of the page, "Petition for Dissolution of Marriage." What did *that* mean? She returned to the kitchen, where the children were busy doing their homework. She tiredly sat down and read through the first few pages.

In the petition, it looked like James was asking for custody of Sean, but he said nothing about Chelsea. Worse, he requested child support *and* alimony from Mia!

She was floored. What the hell!

I had long before established a relationship with Mia's church, having met with the pastor there to explain the collaborative divorce concept and all of its positive attributes for the family, as well as for the community. He had already sent us several referrals.

I later enlisted his support when I founded the *Collaborative Divorce Pro Bono Project*. So when she approached him again for advice several days after receiving the petition, her pastor recommended that, if divorce was unavoidable, she should consider using our *pro bono* collaborative services. She gratefully agreed and he referred her to us.

Mia was a sturdy young woman, dressed in the light blue uniform of her (part-time) employer, with long curly brown hair she habitually clipped to the back of her neck. She had bright green eyes, and, when I asked, I discovered that her parents had relocated to Tampa from Puerto Rico before they were divorced. I was surprised when we first met that she was able to smile at me; I could tell that she was anxious . . . and angry. But my office is very welcoming, as is Hachi, who deserves the "therapy dog" certification for the sensitivity that she brings to her relationship with each of my clients. So I could see her visibly relaxing.

I seated her on the warm leather couch in my office and took the armchair catty-cornered from it, glancing through the petition.

First, I answered Mia's questions about likely timesharing, how child support is computed, and whether James might really get alimony or his attorney's fees from her. I explained, "The petition is a form that almost everyone uses. It's unlikely that he really expects to get majority timesharing or alimony from you. In fact, the Florida legislature recently passed a law that suggests that 50/50 timesharing will be the norm from now on. His attorney, not James, probably felt compelled to demand all that stuff, just in case."

She was adamant about what she'd agree in regard to timesharing. "He isn't a homework Dad. I won't let him have Sean school nights; I'll let him have all the weekends, but I have to make sure that Sean gets his homework done. School is too important."

I let that go for the time being, and we discussed how the collaborative process works and whether he might be willing to try it. He'd retained an attorney with whom I had worked cooperatively in the past, so I called her right then and there. With Mia's permission, I suggested that I sit down with both Jackie and James to explain the collaborative divorce concept. Jackie agreed.

I had lunch with Jackie first so that I could pitch her the idea before trying to enlist James. Because I present fairly often on collaborative divorce to both lawyer and lay groups, I was able to summarize the basics in just over ten minutes. My passion about this work is obvious, and I could see the motivating effect on Jackie; she was getting excited.

She's already heard about the disqualification requirement, but the team construct was foreign to her, so she had some questions. We talked about the roles of the neutral facilitator and the financial neutral at length before Jackie, hesitating, asked me, "How would you feel about working with me on the team?"

She hadn't been trained collaboratively, nor had she worked any collaborative cases. I hadn't had any training before my first case either, but that was many years ago, when it wasn't as available as it is now.

"Jackie, our past cooperative cases convince me that you are perfect collaborative attorney material. I'd be happy to mentor you through your first case, if you'll agree to attend a basic training as soon as possible. We can agree on two neutrals who've had collaborative experience, as well. So they'll be able to guide you, too."

I mentioned several volunteers in the *Pro Bono Project* who could work on the Nation team, if James and Jackie agreed to proceed collaboratively.

"What about the fact that we've already filed a petition?" she asked. "The judge has already scheduled the first case management conference!"

"If James agrees, we can 'freeze' the litigation and proceed collaboratively by filing the appropriate stipulation. Our local judges have already agreed to that procedure in an administrative order." I thought for a moment. "Wait, I'll e-mail you a copy. You'll want it for your records." I used my cell phone to take care of that.

By the time I met with Jackie and James, it was clear that she had already sold him on the idea. I think he just wanted to see what I was about before signing on the dotted line. I grasped his hand firmly, while saying warmly, "James, it's so good to meet you. I want to thank you for giving me this opportunity to explain the collaborative divorce concept to you for your consideration. Mia has already agreed to it, but it takes both of you to agree. If one spouse doesn't agree, the default divorce is the traditional trek through the courtroom and that can get ugly."

He wasn't much taller than Mia, perhaps 5'8", but he wasn't Hispanic; he was a handsome, well-built black man, about 34 years old. He seemed surprised that I was so friendly. Perhaps he had different expectations? I *was* the "opposing lawyer," after all.

We talked in Jackie's conference room. She asked more questions than he did (James turned out to be very reserved), but they were true "softballs," inquiries designed to allow me to get my points across. She also offered him some true-life examples of the horrible things that had happened in some of her court cases, completely beyond her and her client's control.

Ultimately, he agreed to collaborate, and Jackie and I assembled the team. We agreed on a facilitator, Gavin, as well as a financial professional, Michelle, who was well known in the divorce community, both in court and out. Jackie had used her in court. I had worked with both on collaborative teams and they were both volunteers in the *Pro Bono Project*. We decided that our

167

clients would not need any other professionals, at least not initially.

I sent both neutrals my "welcome to the *pro bono* team" e-mail, and received the requisite, "count-me-ins."

With the team in place, Gavin and the clients scheduled their initial interviews. Soon after, he sent his report to the rest of the professionals, and we discussed it at our first teleconference. Here are the pertinent portions of what Gavin shared with us about James:

Trust Issues: [Level of trust (1) = no problems and (10) = virtually impossible]

- James' overall level of trust for Mia was a "4" and a "5" related to the children.

Parenting Issues/Concerns:
- Parallel parenting style
- Very limited and poor communication between parents
- No routine or consistency in their co-parenting
- Believes their goals for their son are the same

Communication Style:
- James stated his communication with Mia was "horrible." They currently have very little interaction with each other. Information appears to be conveyed through their son or the occasional text message. According to James, they had a better relationship prior to this summer. He recalled being able to eat dinner together and carpool to his son's games. He wasn't sure what happened over the summer, he just knew that it abruptly stopped.
- James stated he often doesn't show his stress or anger. He works hard to control his emotions because he has a "bad temper" and doesn't feel others can handle him when he is upset.
- He thinks his lack of emotional expressiveness may bother others and definitely upset Mia when they were together. He feels she wanted him to show more emotion in their relationship.

- When he feels he is getting emotional, he'll ask for a break or walk away from an argument.

Conflict Resolution:
- James described the following pattern when the clients were together. One of them would bring something up, the other person would state their rebuttal, and then it would lead to a verbal argument. As a result, James found himself frequently trying to avoid arguments.

Expectations of the Collaborative Process:
- James wants the divorce process to be over and is willing to compromise to reach an agreement. He felt they would be able to sit in the same room with each other without incident and was confident they could get through the process successfully.

And here is what Gavin shared with us about Mia:

Trust Issues: [Level of trust (1) = no problems and (10) = virtually impossible]
- Mia trusts James with the safety of their son, but she doesn't trust him to tell her the truth.

Parenting Issues/Concerns:
- Parallel parenting style
- Mia concurred with James that their relationship changed significantly over the past few months. However, neither verbalized a reason for this dramatic change in their co-parenting.
- Prior to separation they were on same page, but since that time, James rewards Sean and doesn't support Mia with decisions she makes in her home or with Sean's behavior outside the home.
- In contrast to James' observations of his son, Mia described Sean as always being a happy kid prior to their separation. Since that time, he's been crying more frequently, is less respectful at home and school, and blaming Mia's friend

(she had a new romantic interest) for the divorce. He's even been disrespectful to his football coaches, which is out of character for Sean. She believes Sean is attempting to split the parents because they don't communicate.

Communication Style:
- During the interview, Mia initially presented as guarded. Once rapport was established, she openly shared the difficulties she's had during and after their marriage, specifically with being able to co-parent with James. The team should be aware that Mia appears to be holding in a great deal of anger and frustration with James. She's likely to try to keep her emotions contained, but is at risk of becoming upset quickly as we begin to address unresolved issues in the team meeting.
- Mia described her relationship and communication with James as almost non-existent. She tries not to use their son as a messenger. However, Sean goes back and tells his father everything that happens in her home. She wasn't sure if James was encouraging this behavior, but it's been causing stress in her home.

Conflict Resolution:
- They are not able to resolve their conflicts. Therefore, they do not talk.

Expectations of the Collaborative Process:
- Mia was confident that they would successfully get through the collaborative divorce process.
- Mia identified the need to improve their co-parenting and communication skills as her greatest hope for this process.
- Mia wants James to "change" for their son.
- She added that her greatest fear, regarding the divorce, was James trying to (legally) take their son away from her.

Communication and trust were both clients' biggest problems. Because of this, they had never learned to effectively communicate with one another.

Mia could be short-tempered and blunt at times. She was very angry and frustrated with James. She tried to keep her emotions contained, but often became upset.

James had trouble trusting other people to be there for him when he needed help. Consequently, he had limited relationships; he identified his mother, aunt, and brother as his primary support system. He believed that he had a bad temper, so he worked hard not to show his stress or anger and to control his emotions. Although he understood that his lack of expressiveness upset her, when he felt himself becoming emotional, he'd remove himself from the situation. He often avoided confrontation altogether.

What did the clients agree on? Although they were unaware that they were of the same mind, they both felt that their relationship had changed significantly over the past few months. Neither seemed to know why. She felt that it might have been because he believed she was involved in a new relationship. However, Michelle shed a different light on the issue when she suggested, during our first professionals' teleconference, that it was because James had recently completed a loan application when purchasing a new car, and Mia happened to see it. She, at least, was upset by the income he was reporting, considering how little child support he was paying her, and the fact that he was supporting his mother, his brother, and his aunt.

Michelle knew this because she, too, had already had her initial meetings with the clients to discuss the marital finances.

Regardless of the cause, this change in their relationship seemed to impact most on their ability to co-parent. James became less willing to support Mia's parenting and discipline. Their already poor communication skills worsened. They each tried to avoid the other, passing information through Sean or the occasional text message or e-mail.

Although Chelsea was not legally involved in the divorce, both parents understood that she was part of their family system and had been negatively impacted by their separation. Mia was especially upset because James' family had cut off all contact with Chelsea, hurting the teen badly. However, James considered Chelsea his daughter and promised he would be there for her whenever she needed him.

During their separation, James had maintained a good relationship with Sean, seeing him every week and Face Timing with him often. Sean expressed concern to both parents that James wasn't visiting with Chelsea. He also indicated that he believed he was the cause for their divorce. Although Sean had always been a happy kid, in the last few months, as mentioned, he had been crying and acting out more frequently, and behaving less respectfully. And he used his parents against one another, although they were unaware of it, for the most part, because of their failure to communicate.

We knew restructuring this family wasn't going to be easy. Jackie and I had lunch again before the first full team meeting to discuss how we would interact in front of the clients.

"My biggest concern is that James will need to see you being his advocate," I started the conversation. "Otherwise, he'll lose faith in the process right away. He can't see you deferring to me because I'm your mentor. By the same token, remember that this isn't the same type of advocacy as in court. We simply need to communicate our clients' interests well with each other, so that they can see how people can disagree but still communicate respectfully and without losing their tempers. And in doing so, we may find common ground."

"I'm not worried about that," Jackie said. "I'm more concerned about James' need for control. He's the hero in his family, and he's used to being in the driver's seat." She cocked her head, quizzically. "So how do we tell him he's going to pay child support, it's going to be in this amount and he'll pay it on the first of the month, without fail, etc. etc. etc.?"

"Let's play that by ear. But you should mention it to Gavin before our first full team meeting." I didn't know how accurate Jackie's prediction would be; after all, she's not a psychologist. But then again, neither am I. And how often do I give emotional advice to my clients? It seems like I say "I'm not a psychologist but . . ." at least three times a week.

James hardly uttered a word during the first full team meeting. That concerned me. He stared at his hands, folded in his lap. Sitting across from him, all I could see was the crown of his head. The longer this went on, the more upset and vocal Mia, sitting next to me, became. At one point, she couldn't express her frustration so she stormed out of the meeting. This was at the end of the two hours scheduled, so we adjourned.

When Gavin raised the timesharing issue at the second full team meeting, Mia immediately took the position that she wanted a vast majority of it. After all, this was how the clients had been operating since their separation, and she would not budge on that issue. But James had already conveyed his desire for more time to his lawyer, and Jackie did a good job making that clear to the team. She and I went back and forth for a short time.

According to Jackie, "Both parents are equally capable of parenting their child."

I pointed out, "But these parents have established a routine that's working for them and their child." (We hadn't yet raised the Chelsea issue.)

Jackie replied, "That's just because Mia has controlled the timesharing and James didn't want to fight with her over it."

At this point, Mia exclaimed, "How can you say that?! I told him he could visit with the kids whenever he wanted. He's the one who hasn't followed through! He's the one who's ignoring Chelsea! He's the one who hasn't paid me any support!"

During her tirade, I reached out and put my hand on her arm. She was working herself up and, when we'd met, just before the full team meeting, she'd asked me to keep an eye on her anger level. I wanted to remind her of that, without actually saying anything. But when she finished, she just seemed to run out of words.

Instead, shaking her head angrily, she leapt out of her seat and ran out of the conference room, out of the office, out into the 95° heat in the parking lot outside. I asked the team to excuse us and followed her out, without stopping for my keys.

"Why doesn't he understand?" she cried, already in tears. "I need help; I can't do it all myself anymore! Why doesn't he know that?"

I put my arms around her. I am not usually a demonstrative person, even in my private life. But Mia needed to know that someone understood who she was and how it felt to be her. "He doesn't understand because you don't explain. You need to explain."

"He won't listen to me!"

"How do you know," I asked, still holding her tightly, "if you haven't given him the opportunity to listen? First let him speak his piece, then it's your turn. Don't shout; just talk. We'll all listen."

She was silent, her body stiff, but she was thinking. Then she surrendered, "Ok, I'll try."

So I waited a beat and then I asked her for a favor. "Next time you run out of the conference room, can you head into my office instead? It's a lot cooler in there."

She laughed.

We headed back into the office. Once someone opened the door (I had locked us out) and we reconvened the team, I mentioned that the reason Mia wanted all school nights was because "James is not a homework Dad."

He just slowly shook his head, and Gavin suggested that we table the discussion and talk about their failure to communicate.

James looked up. I think it was the first time I'd seen his face since shaking his hand when he arrived. Mia first voiced her concern about both children dreaming of a reunion between James and her. "This is why I don't talk to James anymore. Sean has told me that he wants us to get back together and I don't want him to have false hope."

I put my hand on her arm. "Mia, don't you realize it's not healthy for Sean to be your messenger?"

It was at this point that Gavin took over the conversation. He discussed with the clients their shared belief that they should not act friendly towards each other because then their children might hope for reconciliation. He explained, "While every kid of divorced parents fantasizes about reconciliation, far more damage is done by parents acting coldly and refusing to communicate with one another. The parents should model the behavior that they want for their children, and this absolutely includes how they treat one another."

It was clear that this comment hit home with both them; they both loved Sean passionately.

Gavin suggested that they might not be aware that, if they didn't communicate, Sean would play them against each other. "So ma

tell me about problems with Sean's homework," he requested.

"I'm a stickler for homework," Mia chimed in. "I refuse to allow him to turn in a shoddy assignment." She continued, "James is too lax about Sean's homework." She showed us pictures on her cell phone of an assignment that James had helped Sean prepare. Although she was disappointed by it, after passing her cell phone around the table, the team agreed that it looked fine. We gently suggested that she was being overly critical.

When James realized that he had the team's support, he suddenly leaned forward and defended himself, "I grew up with parents, aunts, and uncles who were all school teachers. I understand the importance of school. I do Sean's homework with him, when I know he hasn't done it."

He reminded me of an anecdote I had often shared with my friends. "I know what that feels like. I'll never forget when I was in eleventh grade. My mother shredded my book report on *Silent Spring*. And not just once. She made me re-write it again and again until she was satisfied with it." The room was quiet, listening. "I ended up hating that book, but I got an A on the paper." I smiled ruefully.

In response, he told the most amazing tale.

"When I was in the fifth grade, I got this writing assignment. It was during the spring that year, when I was living with my aunt because my mother was working too hard to be really hands on with my brother and me. So we were living with my aunt, but she was a public school teacher, too, so she was just as hard on us as my mother was. Anyway, I wrote this paper and my aunt tore it to pieces. She made me re-write it over and over. I thought she'd never be happy with it. Eventually, though, I guess it was good enough and she let me turn it in and I got an "A" on it." But that wasn't the end of his story.

"So when I got to the eleventh grade," he recalled, "I got an assignment that was identical to the assignment that I'd been given in the fifth grade. So I took my old paper (yes, I still had it), and I rewrote it (with more grown up words, of course), and I turned it in. It was written so well the first time that I received another "A" for it in eleventh grade!"

Her mouth fell open. She's never heard this story.

He then divulged the story of the assignment Mia had criticized. It turns out that Sean had been telling him that he was completing the assignment after school with another student. Mia was stricken by that information. "Sean assured me that you and he were getting the assignment done."

You could tell from the look on his face that this also dismayed him. His failure to communicate with Mia (and hers with him) had caused the problem! But when they spoke about Sean, both clients lit up and were equally engaged. And, with the entire team advising them that it was still important for them to display a united front to Sean, they finally seemed to understand.

When Gavin gently brought up his 50/50 recommendation for the timesharing schedule, the team was shocked that Mia easily agreed to an equal split, after confirming that James was aware of the school's website, where he could check on Sean's homework assignments and he promised her that he would do so.

We moved on to child support. Mia was too proud to ask for more money, but she desperately needed it. She wanted to be independent, but she was resentful that James did not realize their need. Nevertheless, she remained quiet. I had asked her to bite her tongue and see what the team could do for her. Michelle put it out there, "Mia simply isn't bringing in enough to pay all of her bills. And she's not living above her means, at all."

I clarified "James hasn't given Mia any money for the last six months and she needs his help."

No one said anything at first.

James did not point out that Chelsea wasn't his child . . . but he *was* contemplating his hands again.

Michelle saw her opportunity to help and remarked, "I've computed the child support, assuming that the Nations would share time equally with Sean. Because Mia hasn't been able to get a job that pays as well as him, James would owe her $346 per month."

I could feel the resistance radiating off of him. I could practically hear him thinking, "Don't you dare hold my feet to the fire. You can't tell me what to do. Don't try to force me to do anything. I'll take care of my kids my own way."

So I asked, "James, I know you've got some serious financial obligations already. You're taking care of your mom, your aunt, and you're providing your brother with free room, as well. Chelsea's not your daughter, so you aren't obligated to pay for Chelsea. How much support do you think is reasonable to help her out?"

"Why does it have to be in the agreement?"

Michelle interjected before I could. "Once you are in the court system, you're required to file the child support guidelines worksheet. And the final judgment is required by law to include statutory child support, unless you provide good enough reasons for the support to be different than the statute specifies."

You could see James chewing on that. Michelle was neutral; he had no reason to distrust what she was telling him. And Jackie was nodding her head in agreement.

"How about $500 a month?"

Although it had begun as a heated conversation because she felt that he wasn't giving her enough money, her mood quickly changed when it became clear that he was more than willing to do his fair share, in fact, even more than the child support guidelines required.

When I asked how he wanted to handle the six months when he'd not paid her anything, James spoke for himself, cutting Jackie off.

"How much can you afford to pay, over and above the support itself," I asked, discretely reminding him that he'd be paying the support, too.

"I'll pay her an extra $200 a month," he suggested. "But I only owe her for five months, not six."

Mia was busy on her cell phone, checking her bank records, so I asked, "Do you know when you'd like to have the total paid back by?"

"I'll have Mia paid by Mother's Day." The symbolism of that date was not lost on her or the rest of the team. It was a lovely gesture.

In the meantime, she confirmed that he had only missed five months, not the six I had mistakenly thought.

That brought us to the conclusion of our second full team meeting. Because the clients had separated years earlier, neither of them expressed a need to discuss personal property or alimony, or any other issue, for that matter.

We scheduled one last meeting to sign their settlement documents. Afterwards, I interviewed Mia for her opinion on collaborative practice and her divorce. I asked what she had feared most, walking into the process.

"My biggest fear was that we wouldn't be able to agree to anything." She paused and then continued, wonderingly. "I was surprised that we were able to listen to each other as well as we did." She smiled and shrugged. "I really credit the team for being so active in helping us *hear* each other. It certainly sounds different when someone else says it, even when it's the same thing my husband just said. Especially when the someone who repeats it is someone I respect."

"But it was not the battle I expected; it wasn't at all hostile," she went on. "That was so weird!"

"Part of that is the safety of the team," I commented. "We're all listening and being part of your conversation. So, not only do things sound different when someone else says them. But they also sound different when all of us are listening. You suddenly hear things differently through someone else's ears."

"Absolutely. It made it easier for him to hear me out, and for me to hear him out. To really 'hear' each other. I was able to say what I needed to say about how I really felt and he 'heard' me."

She continued, "That first meeting especially was a roller coaster, not knowing what to expect. I still remember what you said, when I stormed out the second time, so angry and so frustrated. 'Just come back and talk; say what you have to say. We will listen to you.' I trusted you and, even as unsure as I was, because I trusted you, we still accomplished something at that meeting."

"I learned how to communicate with him, to wait it out, to calm down, and to think about the words I could say that would make our discussion better, instead of worse. What you say sounds a whole lot different when your whole team is listening."

"You know, when we started the process, we didn't talk at all anymore. I would only text and e-mail him. I was so angry at him, and I didn't want to fight. And I knew that we would. But now I think we can work these things out."

I changed the subject. "What surprised you about the process, if anything?" I was careful not to suggest an answer.

"I was amazed that I got what *I* wanted and he got what *he* wanted."

I laughed out loud; I couldn't help it. "What are you talking about? You were so adamant about not letting him have school nights! Remember? 'He's not a homework Dad' and all that?" I imitated her.

"Well, ok, what I wanted changed during the process. So I did get what I wanted in the end," she conceded.

I waited.

"I was also amazed by the atmosphere in the room. We were all on the same team, all of the neutrals, the lawyers, and us, just working hard to get the issues resolved."

She was so right! It is not often that a client learns valuable life lessons, especially when it comes to co-parenting and communication. But when clients choose to collaborate, rather than to litigate, this is often the pleasing result.

Chapter Thirteen

Resolving Child Issues

Collaborative dispute resolution presents an ideal process for resolving issues related to minor children. A primary goal of this method seeks to ensure that the parents establish or maintain a good relationship with one another once they have resolved their marital disagreements. Children need their parents to at least manage a working relationship with each other. Litigation can destroy that foundation because parties are forced to be adversarial and to "duke it out" in a hostile environment, the courtroom.

Alternatively, the team setting affords both parents the opportunity to discuss their issues in a safe place, surrounded by professionals whose sole purpose is to assist them in reaching an agreement that best meets each one's most important interests.

If the disputes only relate to the children, the team may dispense with the financial neutral professional, and instead have each party's attorney and the neutral mental health facilitator. They may also include a child specialist, who specializes in the developmental stages of childhood and can best help formulate a parenting plan. It still may be beneficial to retain a neutral financial professional to assist with issues such as child support, health insurance, uncovered medical expenses, planning for college, life insurance, tax deductions, and other financial matters regarding the children.

Many collaborative participation agreements include language that the parties agree to consider their children's best interests and to only communicate with each other in ways not detrimental to the children. They agree to be "transparent" in this regard, which ensures open discussions regarding the children.

In this setting, the team professionals can cover any issue that the parties raise for their consideration and are not restricted to the few issues that a judge is allowed "by law" to decide. They are able to craft their parenting plan in as much detail as needed.

Most often, the parents will share parental responsibility, taking part in decision-making for the children. Judges generally only order ultimate or sole parental responsibility in extreme situations, such as domestic violence or child abuse cases. Those who choose collaborative divorce have more freedom to openly discuss the children's best interests. If they get along well enough, they may wish to divide the decision-making, especially regarding health, education, religion, extra-curricular activities, and any other issues unique to their family.

People who reach a well-thought out collaborative agreement are less likely than litigating parties to have post-judgment issues. Because they take ownership of their collaborative agreements, they're more likely to abide by them. And, if circumstances do change, necessitating a revision to the parenting plan, they can reconvene their collaborative team to address those problems.

Many parents can't conceive of the long-term impact their quarrels can have on their children. But impact they do. Ask any adult child of divorce, if her parents' divorce was contentious.

Perspective

I empathize with the true victims of the traditional courtroom divorce. As I've mentioned already, I was seven years old when my parents divorced. My mother promptly relocated us kids from Los Angeles to New York, and I never saw my father again.

Later, whenever I would ask for something that we couldn't afford, Mom explained that my father never paid his child support, and I therefore couldn't have it, unless I earned the money for it. That was "truth" for me. I never questioned it.

In retrospect, I suppose, this "truth" made me a more independent person at a younger age than I might otherwise have been. I was pretty much on my own financially from the age of sixteen, although I had student loans that my stepfather guaranteed on my behalf, but I ultimately repaid.

We lived with her parents in my mother's childhood home in New Rochelle. Every weekday morning, she caught the train into Grand Central to her job in the city. Until then, she had been a stay-at-home mom. Now my grandmother took over, raising her daughter's four little girls. My grandmother had already raised her family, and she always deferred to my mother when it came to parenting issues.

At nineteen, in my last semester at Yale, my father telephoned me. This was well before cell phones, and, even today, I have no idea how he got the phone number for the dormitory room, but there he was, on the phone. No caller ID, back then, and I had just picked it up. I recognized his voice, despite the years.

He asked how I was, and talked as if there had not been twelve years of my very short life intervening, as though we had spoken just the month before. On the other hand, I remember how baffled and proud he was that his eldest daughter was about to graduate from an Ivy League college.

I was so surprised I don't remember much else about the conversation. I only recall it was extraordinarily mundane. Afterwards, I regretted that I hadn't thought to ask him why he had never called before. (Actually, I've regretted not asking him a lot of things, over the years.) We made no arrangements to talk again.

I called my mother soon after. As I've mentioned before, I was a mama's girl, and she was, after all, my best friend.

"Why do you suppose he called me?"

"I don't know, Honey. I suppose he wanted to know if you were supporting yourself. After all, the age of majority in California is 21 years old."

"What do you mean, 'age of majority?'"

"Well, he probably wanted to know if he still had to pay child support. If you were supporting yourself, then he could argue that he didn't need to."

"Oh, I get it." As per my usual, I accepted the gospel from my mother's mouth. When you only have one parent, you learn not to question her truth. Not consciously; the lesson is subliminal. A child is so dependent on his parents. When he only has one, that dependency is utter.

Two parents offer greater insight, "depth perception," if you will. Their differences and disagreements teach their child that reality has a certain flexibility, that two people can see the truth very differently. Each parent tempers the other; it's like the difference between having one eye and having two. You can see with one eye, but you don't have any depth perception. Two eyes give one perspective.

I was forty-seven before it finally struck me – the discrepancy between what I believed and accepted as fact versus my mother's justification of why he had called me. My insight dawned while I explained to one of my client's why she needed to foster her child's relationship with *his* father. I was describing how sad it was to grow up without a father, knowing he had paid no support, having no contact for years, and then only a single call. I heard myself say "and he was only calling because he didn't want to pay child support anymore."

What?

Had he paid child support for me? I'll never know. My mother and I don't speak anymore.

You can't possibly forget some cases particularly those involving child abuse. Thankfully, justice prevailed in this case, despite that it was a traditional courtroom process. But the client is still paying me, years and years later.

The Sisters

Amber Taylor came to our firm with an absolutely gut-wrenching story. At the time, she was just shy of thirty years old, and already divorced from the father of her two little girls. Although she looked young for her age, there was a maturity to her that convinced me she'd already experienced a lot of heartache. When she first came to us for advice, she was anxious, for reasons that became apparent later, but she offered a ready smile and had a lot of questions, most of them written down. She was accompanied by, not only her second husband, a quiet man who seemed happy to remain in the background, but also her two daughters. I don't usually permit parents to bring their children with them to consultations, but I made an exception in this case.

Her oldest daughter, Shayla, a ten-year old, was a portly little thing. Although Shayla looked tough, she was a sweetheart. She was very protective of her kid sister, Laila, who was only eight at the time. By physical appearances, you'd never guess that these two were full biological sisters. It appeared that the only characteristic they shared was the chestnut hair they'd inherited from their mother. Laila was a beautiful little girl. She was very petite, with brown, sun-kissed skin, and gorgeous green eyes. Shayla was shy, while Laila was outspoken.

The girls waited in our reception area, with the books they had brought to read, while Amber and I interviewed each other. She painted the following horrific picture for me.

"My ex-husband, Anthony, is remarried, and the girls spend alternating weekends and occasional weekdays overnight with him." She paused to take a deep breath. "One evening recently, while the girls were at his house, his wife, Lauren, called me. She said that Laila had told her that Anthony had sexually assaulted her."

I was reeling inside, but I replied calmly, "How horrible. What did you do?"

"I immediately went to his house. On the way there, I called him. I was so scared and angry."

"What did he say?"

"He was crying, and he said he didn't know why Laila would say such things. That made me so angry because he clearly wasn't going to confess, he was just going to blame it on Laila."

"What did you do when you arrived at his home?"

"I sent the girls to the car and asked Anthony again, face-to-face, what had happened. Seemingly baffled, he just shook his head."

"By his reaction, did you believe that he hadn't done it?"

"No. I thought then that, if Laila's accusations had been false, he would have been irate, rather than crying and scared."

"Makes sense to me. So what happened next?"

"I took Laila to the hospital where she was interviewed by the staff and Child Protective Services. Laila told them that Anthony had come to her room, pulled down his pants, lifted his shirt, picked her up, and started kissing her all over her body." Amber shuddered. She took a moment before proceeding. "He touched her with his hands around her anus." Amber began to cry, and I passed her the tissues. She proceeded, "he touched himself, and Laila said that white stuff came out onto the floor and her tummy."

I set aside my outrage and reached across the table to grasp her hand. "I am so sorry that Laila had to suffer through this. No child should have to experience this. Did she say whether it had happened more than once?"

Amber sobbed, "Yes, she said that it had happened before. He told her not to tell anyone, but the first time when the girls were at Anthony's home alone after these incidents, Laila told Shayla. Shayla urged Laila to tell me, but they both hid in Laila's closet at her dad's home and called Lauren, their stepmom instead, who immediately called me."

In retrospect, Laila's reporting first to Lauren seems perplexing, as does Lauren's immediately calling Amber, but I tell the story as it happened, not as the reader would think it should have happened.

I gently questioned her. "Do you know whether he has a history of sexually deviant behavior?"

Amber looked down at the floor. "He does. I first discovered that he'd been convicted as a sex offender when I was pregnant with Shayla. He had claimed that the events occurred when he was seventeen and his girlfriend was sixteen. He explained that, after he turned eighteen, he was arrested because she was still a minor. He told me that it was the girl's father who had discovered the extent of their love affair and had come after him, despite his ex-girlfriend's objections."

"Is that really what happened?"

"No. I later learned the girl was only fourteen, resulting in Anthony's conviction for lewd and lascivious behavior on a child under sixteen. As a result, he was forced to register as a sexual offender."

"Has he had any other trouble with the law?

"Yes. Later, he was arrested three times for driving under the influence, and he was sentenced to four years in prison for violating probation. Because of his alcohol abuse, my life with him quickly became a nightmare. I stayed in part because I wanted my daughters to grow up with their father in their lives, unlike me; my own father disappeared when I was very young. As a result, I made every effort to keep him involved; I chose not to report his beatings or his demands for bizarre sexual behavior.

"Anthony spent much of our marriage behind bars. When he was finally released, he asked me to move back in with him with the girls so we could work on our marriage. Despite my disinterest, after much persuasion, I reluctantly agreed, believing this was the best thing for my daughters."

"How did that go?"

"At first, things were okay. Then, when the girls were four and six, while I was at work, he got drunk and left them home alone. I had him arrested, and he was convicted of one count of simple assault and two counts of child endangerment. He was ordered to attend Alcoholics Anonymous classes and anger management courses. I stuck by him through AA and things settled for a while."

"Then what happened?"

"Then he was arrested for possession. I took the children and moved in with my mother, hoping that disconnecting from him and his crowd would help. But he followed me to my mother's and we continued our relationship. During one overnight, two months later, he got into an altercation with my mother when she complained that he didn't work and that I worked too much. He left in a huff, throwing all of his clothing into his car and demanding that the girls and I move back in with him."

"Did you?"

"Yes, once again, I yielded to him."

"So, how did your relationship finally end?"

"I suspected he was having an affair. I was right, and soon after he moved in with Lauren.

"But I never kept the girls from Anthony. Once he and Lauren got a place with room enough for the girls, they began exercising overnight visits, even before I filed for divorce. Once I filed, we worked out a visitation schedule. I trusted the children with him because I believed he wouldn't hurt them. In addition, they love their dad, and I wanted to keep it that way."

"Did you have a good co-parenting relationship with Anthony and Lauren?"

"Yes. The three of us even met together to discuss his drinking and anger issues, and we agreed that Lauren would call me if the girls ever needed to be picked up because their dad had gotten drunk or too angry."

"Did she ever act on that?"

"On multiple occasions. One time, he became furious with his brother and punched out the window of his brother's vehicle. On another occasion, he struck their dog in the eye because she peed on the floor, and then threw the coffee table across the room. So when Laila reported his latest behavior to Lauren, this wasn't the first time she had occasion to be concerned, and she, again, called me right away."

After learning of Anthony's abuse of Laila, Amber filed a domestic violence injunction to protect Laila from her father. The sheriffs' department and Child Protection Services advised her not to let him have any contact whatsoever with the girls.

During Laila's deposition, she drew a picture of her father's penis, and Amber later verified that she had drawn certain physical characteristics of which she would only be aware if she had seen it closely.

With the help of Child Protective Services, we fought hard to eliminate contact between Anthony and both of his daughters. He denied Laila's accusations, and the case dragged on for a year. The state's goal in a dependency action is usually reunification. The state prepares a case plan, and, when the parent achieves designated goals, then timesharing begins again. The process often progresses from certain limitations until, eventually, there are no restrictions.

Obviously, we were very concerned about the girls ever being around Anthony at all, if Laila's accusations were true, even with careful boundaries. But he put up a good fight. He argued that Laila had seen him watching a pornographic video, and that was how she was able to describe the sexual acts and body parts so graphically.

Not long after the girls' depositions, his attorney notified me that Anthony would relinquish his parental rights. I'll never know why, but I've never had a more satisfying day as a lawyer than when I watched him sign away his rights, knowing that neither of these two little girls would ever run the risk of being subjected to his deviant behavior again.

Chapter Fourteen

Overcoming Impasse[6]

At some point in the collaborative process, the clients may reach an impasse that seems insurmountable. If they aren't able to overcome their stalemate, they'll be forced to choose another option to reach that final judgment of divorce. That alternative is litigation 100% of the time, once the collaborative process fails, costing them both much more in money, time, stress, and heartache.

When faced with the possibility of an impasse, the collaborative team will be committed to overcoming it. But what's the process to address the problem of an imminent impasse?

First, define the problem. Is it an emotional or psychological problem? If one client appears to be at the breaking point and threatening to litigate, it's likely his lawyer will first talk with the facilitator to determine a strategy to get the client through the difficulty, and the facilitator should take the lead in addressing it. The client may need additional emotional help.

Is the problem a financial one? If so, the financial neutral should take charge.

Or is the problem a breakdown of the process? The team professionals may need to meet to discuss how it might be resolved, or may bring in another collaborative practitioner as a consultant.

---

[6] Black's Law Dictionary: A point in negotiations in which agreement cannot be reached.

It may also be appropriate to confer with the other spouse's attorney or another member of that attorney's firm.

It may that be one client lacks the knowledge or the skills to deal with monetary matters or career planning implicated by the looming divorce. These can be huge stressors, especially when coupled with the prospect of losing one's spouse, relocating out of one's home, and/or giving up some overnights with one's children.

Perhaps the client needs to be educated about the issue. If the client is missing information, providing the missing information may enable the client to move forward. The financial professional may be able to help one-to-one, or recommend someone with the right background to engage in some personal coaching. Bringing in a specialist at this point may solve the problem. It may be that the team should bring in a neutral vocational evaluator to advise the client in question.

Rarely, but sometimes, the problem arises with one of the team professionals. In this case, the team professionals will all confer to confront the issue. Another collaborative professional may be brought in to mentor the professional who is not quite grasping the process.

Once the problem is defined, it may be helpful to reframe it in such a way that the team can generate options to address that specific issue. Or the team may bring the clients back to their original goals and interests, so that their immediate perspective is brought back to center.

The next step will be to explore the litigation alternative. If you're the client who's ready to throw in the towel, your lawyer will remind you of the perils of litigation. Are you really comfortable relinquishing control of the divorce process to a judge who does not know your or your kids, or share your values? Someone who will make the decisions and enter a judgment controlling your lives at least until your last child reaches the age of majority? Are you ready for the positional, adversarial, and hostile atmosphere of litigation?

Do you understand the inordinate expense associated with the litigation discovery process that, unlike the collaborative process, discourages candor and transparency? Do you fully appreciate how unpredictable litigation expenses are and how often they can escalate rapidly and beyond control? Can you both afford the expense of each of you hiring your own experts who will be used in an adversarial way, rather than sharing one expert? Do you understand that costly post-judgment litigation is more common after litigated divorces than after collaborative divorces because the clients are generally not as happy with their litigated rulings or agreements?

Are you ready for the judge to manage the timetable and for crowded dockets to cause delays? Do you understand that, while litigators fight to win, one side always loses, and usually *both* parties feel as though they have lost? Are you aware that litigation is public and subject to media attention? And that the court process discourages communication between the parties because the lawyers only profit more if their clients are unable to reach an agreement? Do you truly appreciate the destructive nature that the adversarial litigation process has on families?

If you still want to give up on the collaborative process, before you do, take a trip down to the courthouse and spend just one day in a family courtroom. (Divorce court is a public proceeding, after all.) Sit in on another family's divorce process. It's likely to be quite an eye-opener.

Or consult with a trial attorney to get a better idea of what the divorce court process is like. Make sure to take your collaborative lawyer with you; he will ask the questions you won't know to ask.

If you still want to litigate, a fresh face may help. Dependent upon your issues, it may be that both clients should retain a new neutral expert like a financial planner, a business valuation expert, a real estate appraiser, or an estate planner. The clients should agree regarding how the new neutral professional will be chosen, the terms of her employment, whether she may be called as a witness if they are forced to litigate, and how she will be paid.

If you and your spouse still appear to be on the verge of an impasse, your collaborative team should suggest you hire a neutral mediator to try to assist you with your difficult issues. The team will choose one who is particularly skilled at the clients' specific issue, whether that's a lawyer, a financial professional, a mental health professional, or some other type of mediator. The team might choose to use a mediator trained in collaborative practice.

The clients may choose to mediate with just the mediator present, with their lawyers and the mediator present, or with any of the collaborative professionals participating with the mediator. The communications between the clients would continue to be transparent unless a party caucuses, enjoying a separate, private conversation with the mediator.

As always, the process belongs to the clients.

The clients could also opt to submit their specific issue causing the impasse to a private judge or arbiter.

Don't be surprised if your team suggests that the clients may simply need a break from the process. Taking time off to cool off can help each party recover and return more clear headed to deal with the divorce issues.

Even if you have concluded in gridlock, you may take some comfort if you are able to salvage some of the hard work you have performed in collaboration. Consider whether you can enter into a partial agreement regarding any matters to which you *have* agreed. By limiting the number of issues left to litigate, you will save time and money.

Ultimately, it is rare for a collaborative process to terminate in impasse, and it behooves the entire team to work together to encourage the clients to overcome their deadlock.

Let there be no doubt, every divorce has more than two interested parties. Aside from the children, if any, there are also in-laws, friends, business associates, even neighbors, any of whom may have vested interests of varying degrees in the relationship between the two spouses. And, of course, in many cases there are the new "love interests." Many of these third parties offer emotional support. Some get involved by choice or "necessity" and offer financial help. And along with the money comes the meddling.

While stress and emotional fluctuation may cripple decision making skills for the person getting divorced, input from trusted loved ones can help. However, sometimes the support person or the person who pays for the divorce assumes too much control. He may draft motions, briefs, and other documents. She may do legal research, even meeting and corresponding with counsel outside of the client's presence. In some cases, the emotional or economic factor may make the client reluctant to decide without the financier's approval.

Daddy Dearest

I represented Melanie, a beautiful young flight attendant who is still, today, the spitting image of Uma Thurman, a tall, willowy gal with piles of blond curls usually spilling from a clip perched at the crown of her head and trailing down her back. She'd sought the divorce. Her father-in-law's extreme involvement in their lives had

had a severely negative impact on the couple and their young son, and she'd finally had enough.

Gerald, a lawyer and former general, had controlled the parties' relationship from the beginning. Accustomed as he was to his family obeying his wishes without question, he found Melanie's confident, headstrong personality unfeminine. They often butted heads which annoyed her husband, Matt, despite that her strong personality was probably the reason he'd been attracted to her in the first place.

He was a fair-haired, fair-skinned muscular guy, who made a living as a pool subcontractor. I wondered what she'd seen in him, but perhaps I was just embracing her jaded perspective. She'd been struggling in the traditional courtroom divorce process for a year by the time she retained me.

Gerald had been adamant that the couple have a male child to carry on the family name. Prior to Melanie becoming pregnant, Gerald "suggested" that they undergo a gender selection procedure that would sort his son's sperm based on the assumption that sperm carrying a Y chromosome swim faster in a protein solution than sperm with an X chromosome do. Gerald had offered to pay for the entire process.

Melanie was appalled!

When she had announced her pregnancy, Gerald insisted that the young couple determine the child's sex, despite her desire not to know until the birth. Gerald's desire for an heir was that consuming.

Not a week after his grandson's birth, he visited her at home, while Matt was at work. He let himself in with his own key, and found her lying on the sofa with her infant son sound asleep in her arms. Without much introduction, he demanded, "How soon can you get pregnant again?"

When she involuntarily cried out, "Why do you want to know that?!" He was so insensitive that he actually suggested, "You should plan to have a spare."

What?!

She finally filed for divorce when a heated altercation between Matt and her became physical. At that point, they'd only been married for two years and their son was barely a year old. He'd discovered that she'd had a brief affair with a pilot she often worked with *before* they were married but *after* she and Matt had already begun dating.

When their confrontation became violent, she called the police. She retained divorce counsel the following day. She later confessed to me that the attorney had never suggested any courtless alternatives to her, and she had trusted him to "do whatever needed to get done" to get her divorced.

From Day One, Gerald controlled and financed Matt's divorce litigation. We later discovered, he often met with his son's counsel without Matt being present. He paid all Matt's attorney's fees and costs, which eventually amounted to hundreds of thousands of dollars. In addition, he attended most of the hearings and mediations. Even when he was unable to be physically present, he still had his thumb in the pie. During one mediation, we waited while Matt called his father for advice on whether to sign the agreement that he and Melanie had verbally reached. (He did not.)

Over time, Matt had six different lawyers, a virtual revolving door of attorneys. We discovered later that one counsel withdrew because Gerald prepared a letter on the attorney's letterhead, addressed to us, Melanie's counsel. The lawyer refused to send the letter and an argument ensued.

Another pulled out when Gerald presented her with a brief that he had drafted and wanted her to file in one of Matt's multiple appeals. She later testified, careful not to give Gerald a reason to file a grievance against her:

> General Mason [Gerald] provided guidance . . . he wanted input – he wanted to help with the appeal. He was very helpful in getting me all the documents that I needed for the appeal, the exhibit books, paying for the transcripts, which cost around $15,000 all by themselves. He conducted some of his own research and he gave me legal memoranda outlining how he thought I should construct the arguments on appeal.

In clarifying how Gerald had finally, again, stepped over the line, however, she defended herself:

He did want to talk about the case, but I was the one who made the decisions. I prepared the initial brief and, in it, I appealed the issues I believed had merit. After Melanie filed her answer brief, General Mason wanted a lot more input on how I was going to write the reply brief. I just don't allow my clients or their parents to write my briefs or to tell me how to write my briefs. He wanted to do it his way, and I wanted to do it my way. So he found himself another appellate lawyer.

When she was shown the reply brief that the new lawyer had filed, she identified it as the very same document that Gerald had written and that she had refused to file. (Because Gerald wasn't licensed to practice law in Florida, this was arguably illegal, as would have been an attorney's knowingly abetting him in that practice.)

For people with one child, typical minimal assets, and liabilities of a home, cars, and retirement account debt, a divorce should have been a relatively simple and timely matter. This divorce dragged on and was grossly more expensive than it should have been, largely due to Gerald's interference. Instead, the parties had a full evidentiary trial, including a custodial evaluation. In the end, Melanie got majority timesharing with their son. Matt got his pre-marital home. They split their retirement accounts. Then, at least, it should have been over.

It wasn't.

Following the final judgment, life should have settled into a new normal for both of these people. Instead, financed by Gerald and fueled by his legal knowledge, Matt filed years of frivolous motions and challenges. Initially, they appealed the final judgment's award of timesharing, in which Melanie got weeknights, and Matt received three weekends out of four. (Melanie lived 47 miles away in another county, making weeknight overnights impossible.) At the oral argument on appeal, Matt's new lawyer argued that the trial court was simply wrong, and the appellate court should reverse the final judgment, but he wasn't able to offer evidence to support any other ruling. One judge on the appellate panel commented:

> The only way we could reverse would be if there was no view of the law and the evidence that would allow the trial court exercising discretion to give custody of the child to the mother. **I cannot honestly tell you that I've ever done this in twenty years. I don't see how we could do that.**
>
> We clearly have the authority if the court made an error of law or an evidentiary issue to send it back for a new trial, but I'm not certain I've ever seen an appellate court that simply ordered that the trial court was wrong, and that the trial court must exercise its discretion to give the child to the other party.

During the pendency of the appeal, the parties spent thousands of dollars back in the trial court, where Matt was also still filing motions, alleging that circumstances had changed since the final evidentiary hearing and that timesharing therefore should be modified. At one point, this included Matt's motion to disqualify the judge. In support, Matt alleged:

> The Judge has performed multiple violations of law, court rules, or other specific provisions of the Code. [He gave no examples.] The Judge demonstrated her bias and prejudice [because she gave Melanie more time with their child]. The Judge on her own helped Wife by overtly suppressing, and, in effect, hiding of testimonial evidence from the appellate court. [He gave no examples of any such thing.]

When the judge denied this motion for Matt's failure to even allege a prima facie basis for it, I was surprised. I would have thought he'd seize the opportunity to be rid of this problem case!

Gerald eventually chose counsel who didn't mind him running

the show, despite the ethical implications for that attorney. Gerald prepared most of this counsel's pleadings and did much of the legal research. (We were later able to establish this in our request for fees.) He also signed Matt's retainer agreements as his "attorney in fact."

Eventually, the appellate court affirmed the trial court's timesharing plan, but the stress even caused Melanie to develop breast cancer, something she had to hide in fear that, should Matt hear of it, he would use it to allege, yet again, a change in circumstances sufficient to support modification of the timesharing plan.

The legal battle went on. Legal squabbles continued over timesharing, choice of schools, and oddly-worded legal documents prepared by Gerald. The trial court found the inordinate amount of time spent on this case, as well as the dollars expended, "shocking." After over four years of litigation, the court found Matt's lack of cooperation to be more to blame.

What does this case show? It clearly points to a compelling interest for courts to find a reasonable way to curtail third party involvement in finances and ensuing control. More disconcerting is the power imbalance when one side through a third party has the means to vexatiously control and continue the litigation. This forces the underfunded party into a defensive position without the means to pay. Third parties should be deterred and penalized for such "bad behavior."

I filed a motion to hold Gerald accountable, to no avail. The judge clearly understood the issues. As he explained it:

> I don't doubt that General Mason – I mean, I've got it everywhere. He paid the bills, he was here all the time. It seemed like he's a retired guy that loves his son, loves his grandson, and, by God, might be an absolute nut at this point, but definitely spent a lot of time on this. I'll tell you right now. I mean, this is obvious. You don't write stuff like this if you're a good lawyer, if you know what you're doing, if you're objective, which he's not. I mean, he's involved.

In the end, however, the judge couldn't see his way clear to holding the grandfather, who was not officially a party, responsible for my client's exorbitant defensive legal fees. However, he did share his concerns:

> The Court is aware that this decision appears to leave a wrong without a remedy. That it may send a message that a "nonparty" can run amuck in the courts without risk. However, there are other consequences and checks in place. For instance, [Gerald]'s actions have essentially financially ruined his son because he has been hit with tens and tens of thousands of dollars in judgments for attorney's fees and costs. (Understandably, that does not make Former Wife whole for the obscene fees and costs she has incurred having to fight off this wasteful litigation.)
>
> Although I did not try the underlying case involving two relatively young folks who had no meaningful incomes or assets, or extraordinary child sharing issues, it appears clear that this litigation violated the heart of the basis of our civil justice system, which is to "secure the just, speedy and inexpensive determination of every action." I just can't see any legal way to hold [Gerald] accountable for the damage he has caused.

There are cases in which third parties have been required to pay the fees of the party suffering from vexatious litigation caused by the third party. Unfortunately, I wasn't able to find a single divorce case in Florida to support that ruling, and I had a judge who wasn't willing to risk reversal on appeal. And let there be no doubt, Gerald would have appealed that ruling.

Their post-divorce litigation continued for three more years, and then suddenly stopped. Matt's counsel cancelled the next hearing and "went dark."

Melanie called me shortly thereafter to pass along the news her ten-year-old son had brought home from his last visit with his father; Gerald had finally died.

Chapter Fifteen

The "Divorce is Bad" Fallacy

Studies have shown that marriage is good for people. Married folks live longer and have a lower risk of a variety of physical and psychological illnesses than single folks. They're happier with their careers. Getting married directly increases happiness and satisfaction with life, which then leads to improved health. It encourages people to maintain good health behaviors and to implement valuable social support, and offers them a sense of purpose in life.

The benefits of a happy marriage are better physical health, more resistance to infection, and a reduced likelihood of dying from cancer, from heart disease, in fact, from all major killers. It can reduce heart disease because lifestyle factors heavily influence heart disease. Sleep is more regular for married people. Most married people eat a better diet than single people, drink less alcohol, suffer from less stress, smoke less, and suffer from less depression. It also protects you from cancer, and helps you beat it because married people get their cancer diagnosed at an earlier, more treatable stage following up with the recommended therapy over twice as often as singles.

Thus, people live longer if they are in marital relationships, particularly good, satisfying ones. They suffer less anxiety disorders, less psychosis, less post-traumatic stress disorders, and fewer phobias. They even have fewer injuries due to accidents. The health benefits are even greater for married men because, traditionally, married women act as nurturers to them. And married men are less likely to engage in those dangerous activities that they enjoyed when they were single, like drunk driving, promiscuous sex, and unhealthy eating.

As a single male, you are four times more likely to be a victim of violent crime than a married male.

But women also benefit. Many experience better financial support which leads to better health care and safer living environments. Socioeconomically, married people make more money, get promoted faster, and live better than the average single person.

The more happily married, the more health benefits you experience. On the other hand, bad marriages are serious life stressors that reverse any of the above-mentioned gains.

In contrast, divorce is bad for people, both physically and psychologically. Divorced individuals die younger than both folks who never marry *and* couples who remain married. They suffer from cancer, cardiovascular disease, infectious diseases, respiratory illnesses, digestive system illnesses, and other acute conditions more frequently than do single, married, or widowed people. They are far more likely to abuse alcohol and/or suffer from psychiatric illnesses. Moreover, the suicide rate of those who are divorced is almost triple the rate of those who are married, and significantly higher than the rates of those who have never married or who have been widowed.

Divorce is one of the most stressful life events that a person can experience. It is extremely emotional, and generally, expensive. Even the most amicable divorces can be devastating to families, not only to those divorcing, but also to their children, parents, siblings, and close friends.

When the divorce is litigated, individuals, including children, are often forced to pick sides. Sometimes the adults, especially the grandparents or new significant others, find themselves footing the bills, both emotionally and financially. In extreme cases, they can become so involved in the litigation that they might as well be named parties.

In a traditional courtroom divorce, as we've discussed before, spouses are pitted against one another in an adversarial setting.

They are "opposing parties." Even if they are trying to avoid a war, once they hire attorneys, the battle usually begins. Litigators are trained to make the road as bumpy as possible for the opposing party. They are encouraged to hone in on the worst characteristics of a person, bring them to everyone's attention, and then focus on them. Traits that were perfectly acceptable in a happy marriage suddenly become intolerable in a divorce.

Children are helpless victims in the process. While they try to cope with the fact that Mommy and Daddy don't live together anymore, they are often thrown into the middle of the battlefield. Parents seek custodial evaluations in which mental health professionals interview the children and delve into every aspect of the family life and the parents' psychology to determine which one should "win" more time with them.

Spouses file domestic violence injunctions to obtain the upper hand in the custody battle, often resulting in children not seeing one parent for extended periods of time and/or timesharing exchanges occurring at police stations. Such exchanges, of course, are not normal, positive experiences. Children are asked to testify, being forced to pick sides and tell the judge whom they love more. No matter what they say, they betray one of their parents, sometimes both.

Most importantly, judges are charged with protecting the kids, and ensuring that their best interests are met. How are they truly able to do that in an adversarial setting like divorce court, where the parents, caught up in the heat of battle, often lose sight of what will best suit their kids? Many a judge complains that he only sees a snapshot of the spouses' marriage, and is only allowed to weigh the evidence placed before him. When spouses at war present that evidence, it is rarely sufficient to fully educate the judge, who, by the way, is no expert on psychology or relationships or child development or education, as to what will best benefit the children.

Costs go through the roof. Parties spend their children's college funds or their own retirements on attorney's fees. Family assets dwindle, and spouses end up fighting over who will be responsible for what's left, the debt, rather than who will receive the assets.

Health suffers. It is traumatic to live in a constant state of stress and to not know what will happen next in your personal life. A lengthy divorce can have detrimental effects on health that may plague the parties for years after, possibly, for a lifetime.

But there *is* a better way. Collaborative practice is a more holistic approach in which the team considers the entire family and aims for a resolution whereby everyone wins, rather than just one spouse, or no one. While, ultimately, the clients obtain a final judgment dissolving their marriage, it doesn't involve the courts in an adversarial way. It doesn't rely on court-imposed resolutions but, instead, permits the clients to negotiate their divorce issues in an transparent and cooperative, private and professions atmosphere. The process focuses on the future wellbeing of the restructured family.

As you now know, each collaborative professional focuses on his strengths and trainings to help the clients in the most effective and cost-efficient way possible. Collaborative divorces generally take much less time and cost much less money than traditional litigated divorces. Furthermore, clients are usually able to maintain positive relationships with one another and to learn skills that will help them communicate and interact constructively with one another going forward.

If you have not been lucky enough to choose a partner with whom you can continue to have a happy marriage, then, to preserve your long-term health, either fix your unhappy marriage, or, if that is not possible, leave it. The divorce option you choose can have a long-term impact on your health. If divorce is inevitable, choose a healthier alternative. Choose courtless. Choose collaborative.

I always tell my clients "I don't approve of divorce." There's some shock value there, as I *am* a divorce lawyer. It gets their attention and they tend to listen pretty carefully to whatever follows. But it's not as absolute as I make it sound. Obviously, there are situations in which divorce is the best, indeed the *only* solution to the problem.

I, myself, am divorced. And there's a good reason why.

The Thief

I was married on Valentine's Day, less than two weeks after my 30th birthday. I had decided that I was headed for "old maidhood" if I didn't get married soon, and my boyfriend at the time was a charming lawyer with an attractive personality who had wooed me unremittingly during the seven months leading up to our wedding.

Unlike women who dream about babies, I imagined practicing law with him some day in a firm of our own.

After our marriage, however, his disposition seemed to do an about-face. He transformed from a running, swimming, biking athletic Ironman into a pudgy, overweight sloth who spent his evenings spread out on the couch watching the boob tube. I'm not kidding; he gained 50 pounds in six months.

There were days when he would come home from his law office, located just six floors below mine in the same downtown skyscraper, with a roll of hundred dollar bills concealed in his jacket pocket. I would find thousands of dollars rubber-banded together back when "a thousand dollars" was a big number. He didn't seem to care that I had assumed responsibility for taking clothes to the dry cleaners, that I would invariably check all of the pockets for money and important documents, receipts, or notes before I dropped it off.

What was that all about? When I asked, he simply said he hadn't made it to the bank before it closed.

Then he asked my secretary to notarize a signature when she hadn't witnessed the individual sign or verified his identity, both required under the law. When I told him she couldn't do that, he seemed honestly surprised. Perhaps he was just unfamiliar with that prerequisite?

But it wasn't until I caught him emptying my wallet fairly regularly behind my back that I recognized the magnitude of the problem. I didn't have the education or the experience back then to determine how best to handle the situation myself, so I consulted with a licensed mental health counselor.

It didn't take her terribly long to announce, "I think that the real problem here is your husband. He's a sociopath." She explained, "Given all of the symptoms that you've described, assuming that they are all true, you can't fix that problem. He will never understand why you feel that cheating is unacceptable, stealing is wrong, lying is offensive, and unethical behavior is intolerable."

I sat in front of her desk, my hands clasped and my fingers laced, with my elbows on my knees. I stared at the floor, willing the tears to drain away. She went on, "sometimes you just have to know when to give up." She smiled ruefully. "I'm so sorry."

I didn't know what to do. I had meant "for better or for worse," hadn't I?

Then came the day when I discovered that he had sold our home out from under me. Shortly after our wedding, after I moved in with him, he had asked me to pay the mortgage. It was an unpleasant surprise to discover, just two weeks after our nuptials, that he was filing a petition requesting bankruptcy protection. Apparently, he wasn't making enough money to pay the mortgage himself. I agreed, but I had asked him to add my name to the deed for the home, along with his own.

"Of course, I will. It's easy. All I have to do is sign a quitclaim deed," he assured me.

I didn't realize that, in Florida, at least, one can only gift real estate from one person to another with the second person's signature. And he never gave me a quitclaim deed to sign.

It wasn't until he had made arrangements to sell the house that I had reason to discover his duplicity.

"Why didn't you put the property in my name like you promised?" I wanted to shout, but I didn't. I was icy calm.

He seemed unconcerned. He shrugged, "I forgot."

"You forgot?!"

"I forgot."

He forgot, despite giving me the mortgage statement to pay every month.

And now he had sold the home and I would have to move. I didn't know where.

That was the final straw. I wanted a divorce.

But I was afraid to say so. So I suggested that, given how disappointed I was that he had "forgotten" to put the house in my name as well as his own, this was a good opportunity for us to spend some time apart, considering what we wanted from the relationship.

Shortly after I moved into my new home, I heard something outside the window. Twigs breaking, leaves crunching. I ran over to the window and peaked outside the curtain. There he was, prowling around in the bushes. I watched him creep from window to window, skulking around the perimeter of the house, trying to see inside.

I walked over to the house phone and dialed his number. It rang and rang, and then his answering machine picked up.

"I want a divorce," I said, and hung up.

Within a week, I came down with *Type 1 Diabetes*, better known as *Juvenile Diabetes*. I had been to the endocrinologist just two weeks earlier, and he had pronounced me fit.

But shortly thereafter, I suddenly came down with a bladder infection. I recognized the symptoms (once a woman has had a bladder infection, she never forgets what it feels like), and I ran back to the doctor, assuming it would be a no-brainer. He'd give me the standard prescription, a tablet that would eliminate the infection and my pain.

Instead, he performed a blood test. "Why is your blood sugar over 400!" he demanded, as if I would know.

"What are you talking about?" I asked. I had no clue.

"The reason you have a bladder infection," he explained, consternation written across his brow, "is that the sugar in your bloodstream is too high. This is usually caused by diabetes. Does it run in your family?" He asked.

"No. What is it?" I had no clue, again.

He explained what diabetes is, and its different varieties. As I wasn't pregnant, it was not gestational diabetes. As I was 5 foot seven and very slender, *and* athletic, it was unlikely to be *Type II Diabetes*, which is usually caused by having an overworked pancreas, and an overweight body.

"Just what is going on in your life?" my doctor asked.

I answered in abbreviated sentences, needing to get the problem resolved as quickly as possible. "I just told my husband I want a divorce. I've moved out of the house. He sold our home without telling me."

"Not only that, but the lawyer on the other side of my federal case just filed a pleading accusing me of being unprofessional. It's just a trial tactic, but it's very upsetting," I clarified, becoming angry all over again, just thinking about it. "It's just a ploy to try to get the upper hand in the case. He's totally misstating the facts."

"But you have to defend against it, right?" he commented, nodding knowledgeably. "So you're under a lot of pressure, and you're distressed." Then he added, "And it's two weeks before Christmas, and it sounds like you're suffering from a cold. Additional stressors."

Ultimately, the doctor insisted that I check into Joslyn Diabetic Center for a complete work up. He didn't know if it was diabetes, but he couldn't think of a more likely cause, and, if it were *Type 1 Diabetes*, then I would need to be put on an insulin regimen right away.

I flew to Boston, to the only diabetic center in the country at the time. (Today, there's one right around the corner from me, in Clearwater.)

There, after three days of poking and prodding, I was diagnosed with *Type I Diabetes*. I attended classes all day, where they taught us how to take care of ourselves. Who knew that diabetics shoot up with insulin every day? That was an eye-opener. They also trained us in appropriate nutrition, regular exercise, and all the other things that a diabetic should know. (Well, they didn't tell us everything; they neglected to warn that one can overdose on insulin if not careful. But that's another story.)

When I returned to Tampa, I got divorced. One of the last things my husband said to me was "You'll die all alone. No one will want someone who's diabetic." It was the most stressful period in my life, at least until that point. Even though my attorney did manage to negotiate an agreement, it still took about ten months from my decision to file until the final uncontested hearing. But I was thrilled to be out of a bad situation.

My secretary scheduled the hearing for Halloween, her idea of a good joke.

Even after we were divorced, it wasn't over. I received a call from the State Attorney's Office, specifically from my old boss, in fact. She wanted me to come down to the office to talk about my former husband.

"What?" I was at a complete loss.

"We have reason to believe he's been stealing from his clients." She was right up front. "I'd like to talk to you about it."

I called my friend, a criminal defense attorney, and asked him for a favor. I couldn't afford to hire an attorney!

It turns out that my former husband had been charged with 34 counts of fraud, perjury, forgery, and grand theft. Apparently, he really did *not* know right from wrong. My attorney explained to the assistant state attorney that, even had I wished to tell them whatever I knew, and he wasn't saying whether I knew anything, my ex-husband's husband/wife privilege prevented me from speaking.

They sent me back home.

My former husband ended up pleading "no contest" to the 34

counts, and he was sentenced to "time served." (This was back before the sentencing guidelines required something more stringent.)

He also lost his license to practice law; he would have to reapply for admission to the bar and only after five years had passed.

I saw recently that he is president of the Tampa Catholic Lawyers Guild. And he has the J.D. after his name on LinkedIn. Well, they can't take away his law degree, can they?

Discussion Questions for Book Clubs

1. What has been your experience with divorce?

2. Did you use the traditional approach or the collaborative process? What would be your advice to others going through the process?

3. What did you do to relieve the stress and pain of the divorce process? If you've not been divorced, what do you do generally speaking to relieve stress?

4. Which story in the book struck a chord with you?

5. Do you have stories from your personal or professional experience to add?

6. How does this book compare to other books that you have read about divorce?

7. Which advantage of using the collaborative process is the most important and why?

8. What else, besides the suggestions in the book, would you be looking for in a collaborative attorney?

9. What advantages or disadvantages do you see for the one-coach model versus the two-coach model?

10. What suggestions do you have for improving

communication between the parties and the professionals involved in the collaborative process?

11.   What suggestions do you have for moving parties from adhering to their positions to working from their interests?

12.   What are your thoughts about involving the children in the collaborative divorce process? When, if ever, is it appropriate? What is the best way to involve them?

13.   Because divorce is a legal procedure, how could the courts facilitate the collaborative process?

14.   What suggestions do you have for expediting the collaborative process?

15.   If there were to be a ceremony at the end of the collaborative process, what would it include or involve?

Please share your suggestions, comments, and ideas with me at Joryn@OpenPalmLaw.com.

About the Author

Joryn Jenkins is an attorney with 35 years of experience in the courtroom. She focuses her practice on courtless divorce at *Open Palm Law*, in Tampa, Florida, and has made changing the way the world gets divorced her mission. Ms. Jenkins received her B.A. from Yale University and her J.D. from Georgetown University Law Center. She is a former editor of *The Family Law Commentator* and the former editor-in-chief of both *The Federal Lawyer* and *The Bencher*, magazines with national circulations. She is the author of *War or Peace, Avoid the Destruction of Divorce Court, The Stepmother's Cookbook*, and *Florida Civil Practice Motions* (LEXIS LAW PUBLISHING).

Joryn represented one of the spouses in the first *pro bono* collaborative divorce completed in Florida. She has appeared on Fox 13, ABC Action News, NBC 8, and Bay News 9, as well as on radio on *The Sam Sorbo Show, Legally Speaking, Ask the Dom*, and *Social Media Today*. She has also been featured in *The Tampa Bay Times, The Tampa Tribune*, and *The World of Collaborative Practice* e-zine, all on the subject of collaborative practice and divorce.

Joryn founded the *Cheatwood American Inn of Court* in 1988, and served in its leadership until after her presidency in 2001. She also founded the *Coordinating Council of Florida Inns* in 1989, and served on the American Inn of Court Board of Trustees from 1991 until 1997.

In 2001, Joryn received the *A. Sherman Christensen Award*, the only award then bestowed in the courtroom of the United States Supreme Court, for ethics, professionalism, and civility.

The Federal Bar Association bestowed its highest honor, *The President's Award*, on Joryn in 1997.

Joryn's Other Books

I Never Saw My Father Again explores the more complex issues of collaborative divorce in depth, and illustrates those precepts with true stories of divorce. If you are interested in a basic examination of the core principles raised in real collaborative divorce cases, look for Joryn's last book, *War or Peace (Avoid the Destruction of Divorce Court)* on Amazon, at http://amzn.to/1C6zGG9. You can also find it on her own website, http://OpenPalmLaw.com/, at http://bit.ly/1DYw79U.

Look for Joryn's next two books, *A Free Divorce Handbook (How to Organize a Collaborative Divorce Pro Bono Project . . . and Why)* and *Changing the Way the World Gets Divorced (Effectively Marketing Collaborative Practice)*.

www.ingramcontent.com/pod-product-compliance
Lightning Source LLC
Chambersburg PA
CBHW052125270326
41930CB00012B/2763